Credit and Collateral

Collateral – generally defined as an asset used to provide security for a lender's loan – is an important feature of credit contracts and all the available evidence suggests that its use is getting more pervasive. This informative book builds upon recent research into this topic.

Sena analyses three case-studies that revolve around the impact that financial constraints have on economic outcomes. In the first case-study, the relationship between firms' technical efficiency and increasing financial pressure is explored. The author then goes on to show, in the second case-study, that under specific circumstances, increasing financial pressure and increasing product market competition can jointly have a positive impact on firms' technical efficiency, while not being true for all types of firms. In the third case, she analyses the impact that finance constraints have on women's start-ups.

Unique and revealing, this is the first book to deal so extensively with the topic of collateral, and as such, is a valuable reference to postgraduates and professionals in the fields of macroeconomics, monetary and business economics.

Vania Sena is currently a Senior Lecturer in Economics at Aston Business School, Aston University, Birmingham.

Routledge international studies in money and banking

Credit and Collateral

Vania Sena

Routledge
Taylor & Francis Group

LONDON AND NEW YORK

First published 2008
by Routledge
2 Park Square, Milton Park, Abingdon, Oxon OX14 4RN

Simultaneously published in the USA and Canada
by Routledge
270 Madison Ave, New York, NY 10016

Routledge is an imprint of the Taylor & Francis Group, an informa business

Typeset in Times by Wearset Ltd, Boldon, Tyne and Wear
Printed and bound in Great Britain by TJI Digital, Padstow, Cornwall

British Library Cataloguing in Publication Data
A catalogue record for this book is available from the British Library

Library of Congress Cataloging in Publication Data
A catalog record for this book has been requested

ISBN10: 0-415-34117-5 (hbk)
ISBN10: 0-203-02347-1 (ebk)

ISBN13: 978-0-415-34117-2 (hbk)
ISBN13: 978-0-203-02347-1 (ebk)

To my mother Silvana

Contents

Tables

Acknowledgements

During the completion of this book, I have cumulated debts of gratitude with the many co-authors and colleagues who have read and commented on previous versions of the manuscript. These include Toke Aidt, Sergio Destefanis, Ornella Maietta, Virginie Perotin and Andrew Robinson. I would like to thank Knox Lovell from the University of Georgia, USA, and Henry Tulkens from CORE, Belgium, for transmitting to me their enthusiasm on the frontier analysis and making themselves available for discussions on my work. I would like to thank Antonio Riti for making available the Mediocredito Centrale database. Last but not the least I would like to thank Mahrukh Umrighar for excellent research assistance.

1 Introduction

Credit rationing is a pervasive feature of the competitive equilibrium in the credit market in both developed and less developed countries. The reasons why this is the case are well established in the academic literature (for a survey of the relevant literature see Gertler and Gilchrist, 1993; Hubbard, 1995); in the credit market, information (about either the future profitability of a project or the creditworthiness of a potential borrower) is distributed asymmetrically between borrowers and lenders (Stiglitz and Weiss, 1981, 1985; Farmer, 1985; Williamson, 1986, 1987a, 1987b; Riley, 1987). Indeed, financial institutions may not be in a position of knowing ex ante either the degree of riskiness of a project (moral hazard) or the creditworthiness of the potential applicant who is seeking funds (adverse selection); therefore they face the problem of devising some mechanism that allows to separate the high-risk applicants from the low-risk ones. In both cases, making the loans costlier (by increasing the interest rate on loans, for instance) may not be a solution; in the case of adverse selection, increases of the interest rate required by the bank may have an adverse impact on the average riskiness of a bank's pool of applicants as these may induce riskier individuals to join the pool of applicants. Equally in the presence of moral hazard, an increase of the interest rate may induce the potential applicants either to choose the riskier projects or to choose an action that can affect negatively the outcome of the project (Williamson, 1986, 1987a, 1987b). Therefore, ceteris paribus, a lender will prefer to ration credit in equilibrium (rather than increasing the interest rate) and not to lend to individuals who are deemed to be risky.

Who will be rationed in equilibrium? A rich literature on the consequences of credit rationing and the impact of the resulting financial constraints has shown that when credit rationing is a permanent feature of the credit market equilibrium, then the financial and personal characteristics of both the borrowers and lenders will affect the demand and the supply of credit and so the characteristics of the equilibrium (Chirinko, 1987; Gertler, 1988; Calomiris and Hubbard, 1990; Chirinko and Schaller, 1995). For instance, in conjunction with the characteristics of the investment project, the borrower's creditworthiness and the size of the collateral that can be offered by the borrower along with both the monitoring capabilities of the lender and the degree of competition in the credit market are all likely to affect the amount of financial resources the borrower will be seeking and how much the lender is willing to lend (Fazzari *et al.*, 1988). A very clear prediction from this literature is that rationed borrowers tend to be firms that either do not have enough collateral to offer as a guarantee to the bank or do not have a long track record in the industry (and therefore can be deemed risky) (Fazzari *et al.*, 1988).

However, credit rationing is not the only consequence of asymmetric information in the credit market. Financial constraints can have additional indirect effects upon which the economic literature has not lingered on long enough. This point was first made by Nickell and Nicolitsas (1999) who have investigated the impact of the increase of financial pressure on several indicators of firms' performance (like total factor productivity, employment demand and so on) using a data-set of UK companies. Their results suggest that increases in the financial pressure can have a positive effect on productivity, although small. The argument put forward by the two authors to explain these results is quite simple and relies on the risk-aversion of the managers that run a firm; indeed they point out that when financial pressure increases, risk-averse managers may want to cut organizational slack so to reduce the probability of the firm going into bankruptcy and eventually losing their position in the company.

More generally, these results obviously indicate that financial constraints generated by the existence of credit rationing of various types clearly alter the types of incentives the economic agents are exposed to and this way, the economic outcomes as well. I conjecture there are two main mechanisms that make this possible: first, I argue that financial constraints act as mechanisms that affect the ex post distribution of rents among the many agents that have contributed to create them. So in this perspective, a tightening of the financial constraints (or even an expectation of an increase in financial pressure) changes (or is expected to change) the way the rents are distributed ex post and if the increase in financial constraints is deemed to be permanent, this will directly affect the behaviour of the economic agents that contribute to the generation of these rents. So for instance consider a firm that is financially constrained as it cannot have access to the full amount of financial resources it requires to fund its productive activities. The direct effect of these financial constraints is obviously the increase of the cost of capital and therefore a reduction in the investment expenditure. However, the impact of financial constraints may be felt more by the managers than by the owners of the firm as the increasing financial pressure may reduce the managers' financial bonuses rather than the dividends to the shareholders. In this case eventually managers may decide to increase effort as long as there is a link between managers' effort and their financial bonuses. So one additional consequence generated by the additional financial pressure is that of increasing the managers' effort in my example. In this case, the distribution of the rents generated by the firm is shifted in favour of the shareholders following an increase of the financial constraints and therefore managers have now the incentive to change their behaviour and contribute more to the firm's activity (by increasing their effort). Second, if an economic agent is financially constrained then this indicates that the contractual relationship between borrowers and lenders is in favour of the lenders so that most of the surplus generated by the borrowers will be appropriated by the lender through the repayments and the interest rates. So, if an individual expects particularly unfavourable credit conditions, then he may decide not to seek external funding altogether and may give up a potentially profitable project. A typical example is the case of self-employment: consider an individual who because of his personal characteristics (gender, personal background, residence in a poor area and so on) expects to be financially constrained (on the basis of some aggregate indicator, like average number of successful loan applicants from disadvantaged areas and so on). In this case, just the expectation of future financial constraints can induce this individual to give up setting up a new company and what is observed in the aggregate is a small number of new firms led by individuals from disadvantaged areas, for instance (or with some specific personal characteristics, more generally).

These considerations drive the overall theoretical perspective that underlies this book. Indeed in this study, I argue that financial constraints can have additional effects on economic outcomes that may not be necessarily negative and all this by influencing the way the surplus (generated either in a firm or in a relationship) is shared among economic agents. Now, if this is a correct interpretation of how finance constraints work, then a few questions emerge that are the central questions of this book. To what extent can a tightening of financial constraints (or the expectation of increasing financial constraints in the future) have a positive impact on the performance of economic agents? This question starts from the observation that several parties in a firm contribute to the creation of surplus in a firm and that these parties (or economic agents) can have different objective functions. So, for instance, workers and managers both contribute to the surplus generation in a firm by supplying effort and managerial skills. Obviously, they will decide to supply the amount of effort that maximizes their own trade-off between leisure and effort; however, the supplied effort may not necessarily be the optimal one from the standpoint of the firm's ownership and this generates what can be labelled "technical inefficiency" in the firm. This problem (known as the "hold-up" problem) is very common in all modern corporations and one mechanism that is commonly used to solve it is by linking the monetary compensation of both workers and managers to the firm's performance. This mechanism creates the conditions for a positive link between increasing financial pressure and firms' performance: indeed an increase in the financial pressure faced by a firm means for both workers and managers a decrease in their remuneration and the only way to counterbalance the negative impact of the shock is by increasing their effort with the additional effect that the firm's organizational slack reduces.

Also, if it is accepted the notion that financial constraints reallocate ex post the generated surplus among the several parties in a firm, then as shown above this implies that financial constraints can be used to re-align the interests of the many agents in a firm to those of the ownership and so this may help to improve the firm's performance. This echoes the effect of product market competition on a firm's performance. So a legitimate question at this point is the following: are financial pressure and state of competition in the product market complementary or substitutes? It is usually claimed that these two mechanisms are complementary as it is usually assumed that the main channels through which they exert a positive impact on firms' performance is by reducing organizational slack; so in this case firms with a higher debt repayment obligation will try to improve their technical efficiency if the competitive pressure is increasing. Therefore the net impact on technical efficiency of increasing product competition and financial pressure is positive. However, the empirical evidence on this point is rather ambiguous. Indeed, increasing competition appears to increase productivity growth in firms with low debt pressure (Nickell *et al.*, 1997). Also, there is no evidence of a positive interaction between increasing product market competition and financial pressure in fostering firms' innovation and then productivity (Aghion *et al.*, 2003). These results have cast some doubts on the extent to which slack reduction is the main channel through which competition enhances productivity: indeed it may well be that in the presence of increasing product market competition the rents earned by the managers may reduce and reduction of the slack may not be enough to offset the reduction in rents (Aghion and Griffith, 2005).

Finally, there exists a rich literature that shows that financial constraints affect adversely the rate of new business formation in the economy in general and of women-led companies in particular. This claim is based on the consistent evidence from empirical studies that shows low levels of involvement in enterprise among women and individuals from minority backgrounds. Indeed, there is a belief that the level of female participation is well below the social optimum and therefore this warrants some government attention. So the argument here is that potential applicants with certain personal characteristics (gender, for instance) may be credit-rationed because of their personal characteristics. This view finds particular support when policy-makers and pundits try to explain the low proportion of female entrepreneurs in most OECD countries as gender is the most obvious personal characteristic that can be used to discriminate potential applicants for external funds. This has provided the background for national enterprise-support agencies (such as the Small Business Service (SBS) in England) to intervene actively in order to strengthen the role of women in the entrepreneurial activity. Also policy-makers across OECD countries have long recognized the barrier posed by the lack of access to credit and designed various schemes to overcome it.[1] While this hypothesis is rather intuitively appealing, the economic literature and empirical evidence on this point is rather ambiguous. Indeed, some authors claim that the indirect evidence in favour of financial discrimination against women is the low rate of approved loans to women-owned businesses once it is compared to that of men-owned businesses. However, there exists some economic literature that claims that it is not gender per se that determines whether or not the applicant will experience financial constraints; on the contrary, it is suggested that this low rate can be simply explained by the fact that usually female applicants are characterized by poor collateral, and limited experience that can have an adverse impact on the profitability of a future company. In other words, once these variables are controlled for, the gender effect should disappear. The literature in this area seems to support this point, as in most empirical studies the evidence in favour of the financial discrimination hypothesis is not robust. So the question is: how really important are finance constraints (or even the expectation of future financial constraints) to explain the low rate of self-employment among women?

I argue that the reason why there is no convergence of opinion over whether women are financially discriminated is because gender and financial constraints interact in a subtler way than first hypothezised. The "financial discrimination" hypothesis as suggested in the literature so far assumes that women apply for funds and then financial institutions either deny them or award them but at worse conditions than applied to men. However, I suggest that financial con- straints work in a different way. Indeed, in my theoretical perspective, finance constraints affect the distribution of rents ex post. If one of the two contractual parts expects that rents will be mostly transferred to the other part, then he will not participate in the relationship. This is not very different from what happens in the relationship between potential lenders and potential borrowers. The debt contract may affect the distribution of the surplus generated by the female entre- preneur and if there is the expectation that this will be distributed entirely or mostly to the lender, then the applicant will prefer not to enter into this type of relationship. In other words, the applicant will self-select him(her)self and will not apply for external funding. So what is observed in the aggregate is a small proportion of loans granted to female applicants. However, what the literature appears to suggest is that once this early stage is overcome, there is no real dif- ference between either female- or men-led companies in terms of access to external funds.

In this book, I discuss and test empirically the relevance of these questions by considering three cases. In the first one, I show analytically the specific circum- stances under which increasing financial pressure can improve a firm's technical efficiency. Then I test the impact of finance constraints on technical efficiency on a panel of firms from Italian manufacturing over the period 1989–1994. In the second case, I show that under specific circumstances, increasing financial pres- sure and increasing product market competition can jointly have a positive impact on firms' technical efficiency. However, this is not true for all types of firms. Indeed, a necessary condition for this to happen is the existence of a link between the firms' performance and the workers' financial remuneration. This requirement is usually satisfied in cooperatives where for organizational reasons the workers receive from the co-op a share of the profits in addition to the wage (whether members or not). Therefore the empirical analysis focuses on the producers' cooperatives where I test whether financial pressure and increasing product market competition can either help or offset each other in improving co-ops' technical efficiency, by using data on producers' cooperatives in the Italian wine industry. In the third case, I analyse the impact that finance constraints have on women's start-ups. I suggest that financial constraints can stop the formation of new business by women. This point has been put forward several times in the literature but here I observe that financial constraints can affect adversely the rate of formation of women-led companies by deterring them from applying for external funds. To test this hypothesis, I estimate a set of self-selection models by using English data on the individuals' intentions of becoming self-employed, drawn from the *Household Survey of Entrepreneurship*, 2003.

The book is composed of six chapters (this one included). In Chapter 2, I analyse the main themes from the theoretical and empirical literature on financial constraints. The last 30 years have witnessed a dramatic revival of research on the impact of asymmetric distribution of information among borrowers and lenders on the optimal properties of the competitive equilibrium in the credit market and on firms' capital accumulation process (Bernanke, 1983; Hubbard *et al.*, 1995; Schiantarelli, 1996). This interest is due to the pathbreaking developments in the economics of information and incentives after Akerlof's seminal paper (1970) on the potential inefficiencies in trade arising when either of the parties involved has an informational advantage. Thanks to a series of influential papers by Stiglitz and Weiss (1981) and Williamson (1986) the formal apparatus devised to analyse trade under imperfect information has been extended naturally to the study of the credit market. They both conclude that informational asymmetries create an incentive problem inducing banks to ration credit. Indeed, in both adverse selection and moral hazard an increase of the interest rate on loans may adversely affect the rate of return to banks and therefore these may wish to hold the interest rate below the market clearing level since raising the rate would lower their returns. Therefore some borrowers will be rationed in equilibrium and will not get enough financial resources to carry out their activities.

Afterwards, a complementary stream of literature (mainly empirical) has analysed the implication of these informational imperfections on firms' productive activities and new business formation, among the others. Indeed, a prediction of these models of credit rationing is that some classes of firms (usually the youngest and smallest) will not get the necessary resources to finance their investments. Therefore a rationed firm's demand for investment will depend positively on its balance sheet position as a strengthened balance sheet implies a borrower has more available resources to either use directly for project finance or as collateral to obtain outside funds. This prediction has been extensively tested and the empirical findings support it generally (Fazzari *et al.*, 1988; Devereux and Schiantarelli, 1989; Hoshi *et al.*, 1991). Equally, the formation of new business will be affected by the availability of personal financial resources of the potential new entrepreneurs. Indeed, when there are financial constraints, external funds may be unavailable or insufficient for the set-up of the new company and this creates a link between the wealth of the potential entrepreneur and the decision to start a business as wealthier individuals will be more likely to start a business. In this context, financial constraints will cause the supply and the demand for credit to be related to the personal characteristics of the borrower; for instance, the borrower's creditworthiness will be judged against some criteria that take into account the personal history of the potential applicant. So, for instance, it is often argued that women from ethnic backgrounds are discriminated against in credit markets. This view is supported by the small number of women-run businesses from an ethnic background that rely on loans from the credit market. This view assumes that lenders reject loans applications from female potential entrepreneurs for a variety of reasons – like lack of collateral (as women do not tend to have control over economic resources), limited education and the unpaid reproductive responsibilities (Goffee and Scase, 1983; Aldrich, 1989) – that may or may not affect the future company's creditworthiness.

This chapter prepares the ground for the following empirical analysis as the key themes from the reviewed literature will be developed in the remaining chapters. Chapter 3 analyses the impact of finance constraints on technical efficiency (or organizational slack) using a sample of firms from Italian manufacturing over the period 1989–1994. The analysis is conducted in two stages. I first consider theoretically the relationship between finance constraints and technical inefficiency and to this purpose I derive analytically the relationship between a firm's technical efficiency and the measure of financial constraints. There are many reasons why a company may appear inefficient but here I assume that inefficiency may be produced by the lack of alignment of interests among different agents working in the firm. For instance, it is well known that because of the split between ownership and control (typical of the modern capitalist firm) managers may have some freedom to pursue their interests (Hermalin, 1992; Martin, 1993) that may not necessarily be consistent with those of the ownership. In my model I assume that managers may decide to enjoy more leisure than it would be optimal for the firm and that therefore the firm will appear inefficient because low effort causes production to be below the maximum effort frontier. In this type of environment, a negative shock to the firm with a consequent increase in the bankruptcy probability will mean for the manager the loss of the financial benefits attached to his position with the firm. In this case, the managers may anticipate these negative outcomes and therefore may decide to increase their effort with the result that the firm's efficiency increases. This theoretical result entails a clear empirical prediction: increasing financial pressure (due to a permanent negative productivity shock, for instance) may induce a firm to improve technical efficiency as long as there exists already technical inefficiency in the organization and there is a clear link between the manager's effort, the financial benefits he receives and the firm's performance. Another way to generalize this result is by considering that a firm that cannot have access to additional external resources to maintain its level of production will try to improve technical efficiency over time to gain productivity. Therefore, I expect that financially constrained firms usually have a better performance in terms of technical efficiency over time than firms that do not experience financial constraints. My model shows that tighter financial constraints create an incentive for firms to improve efficiency. Second, I empirically test this prediction on a panel of Italian firms from 1989 to 1994, divided into eight sectors. The empirical analysis uses frontier analysis techniques that allow firms to compute the firm-specific technical efficiency scores while controlling for the factors that can affect the mean level of efficiency, like the availability of financial resources (Grosskopf, 1993; Battese and Coelli, 1995). The results show that financial constraints positively influence efficiency in most sectors, though it is interesting to notice that the size of the effect varies across sectors and within the same sector according to the measure of finance constraints considered.

Chapter 4 considers again the extent to which increasing financial pressure can induce producers' cooperatives to reduce organizational slack and then to increase technical efficiency over time. However, unlike Chapter 3, I consider whether this relationship holds also in the presence of increasing product market competition. The interest in this type of question is mostly policy-driven. Indeed, if the impact of increasing product market competition is larger the higher the firm's debt repayment obligation, then this indicates that there are non-linearities in the impact of competition policies on firms' performance. It is established that increasing product market competition may work as a disciplining force that again alters the incentive structure of the agents within the firm and as in the case of increasing financial pressure may help to increase technical efficiency. But to what extent may these two forces (increasing product market competition and increasing financial pressure) reinforce each other? These questions are less far-fetched than it may appear. There is an empirical literature that has tried to ascertain whether increasing product market competition and increasing financial pressure are complementary or substitutes to each other. However, the results are not conclusive and this result may be due to the fact that the firms under examination are too heterogeneous and the managers within the firm may have different types of preferences. In this chapter I focus on producers' cooperatives to analyse these issues. The case of producers' cooperatives is quite interesting. It is a well-known fact co-ops suffer from substantial financial constraints and that therefore their profit margins are quite reduced (Hailu *et al.*, 2007); also they have been subject to substantial product market competition as the globalization process has exposed them to increasing competition from foreign companies (Birgegaard and Genberg, 1994). Indeed, there exists a widespread belief that co-ops may not be able to survive the joint exposure to increasing financial constraints and increasing product market competition. Finally, more importantly, cooperatives are a type of organization where for institutional and organizational reasons there is a direct link between the individual financial remuneration (this is the so-called profit-sharing bonus) and the co-op's performance.

In this chapter I analyse these issues in two stages: first I model a producers' co-op and analyse how its technical efficiency varies as it is exposed to a simultaneous increase in both product market competition and financial pressure. I model the producers' cooperative as a specific type of organization where (a) workers have control rights over a specific "asset", their effort, and (b) are paid by a fixed fraction of the overall surplus. The cooperative organizes the production using the workers' effort as an input. In this type of setting, a standard hold-up problem arises (Hart, 1995) as workers prefer to invest in the effort so as to maximize their own expected pay-off from the relationship with the co-op, instead of the overall surplus (that is, both the workers' and firms' surplus). Therefore, the supplied effort is sub-optimal from the co-op's standpoint and so it will appear inefficient, as the actual output will be lower than the potential output (or the output produced by the other firms in the industry that are on the frontier). Suppose now there is an increase in the competitive pressure faced by the cooperative. This may be due to several factors, some of which are related to economic policy (like the reduction of tariffs and other artificially created barriers to entry) and some related to consumers' taste. From the workers' standpoint, this implies that their profit-sharing bonus decreases as well and therefore they may want to readjust their effort to counterbalance the effect of the negative shock on the profit-sharing bonus. However, this will not have any impact on the profit sharing bonus at this stage (as the level of investment is determined in the period before the shock) but it will have an effect on the next period's bonus. These re-adjustments affect the co-op's technical efficiency. As workers increase their investment, the actual output increases and gets closer to the potential output. The result is that inefficiency for the co-op reduces. The mechanism is not very different when I consider the impact of financial pressure on a cooperative's technical efficiency. Workers of a cooperative receive a financial bonus that is proportional to the co-op's realized profits; obviously if they anticipate the possibility that the bonus can decrease following an increase in the financial pressure, they will increase their effort and therefore reduce the internal inefficiencies in the co-op. But what happens when both financial pressure and product market competition are increasing? Our model shows that these two mechanisms reinforce each other (in other words they are complementary): workers care about their wage bonus (in turn a direct function of the co-ops' performance) and they are aware that the joint combination of increasing financial pressure and competition in the product market can erode their bonus. So the logical reaction is again that of increasing their effort in the attempt to preserve their profit-sharing bonus. This will improve the co-op's technical efficiency as well.

Our empirical analysis starts from the two main predictions of this model, namely that increasing product market competition and increasing financial pressure are complementary and that increasing financial pressure is followed by increasing technical efficiency. The structure of our empirical analysis is quite simple. I estimate a one-stage stochastic production frontier where measures of technical efficiency are computed conditional on a set of factors (in our case, state of competition in the product market and financial pressure) that can explain the distribution of scores across firms (Battese and Coelli, 1995). Our data is a panel of Italian producers' cooperatives, specializing in the production of wine, over the period 1996–2001. The results confirm the prediction from the model: the two mechanisms appear to be complementary to each other and technical efficiency increases following increasing financial pressure. I also estimate the impact of financial pressure on the change of technical efficiency. Measures of technical efficiency change have been computed by using Data Envelopment

Analysis (DEA, henceforth) (Banker *et al.*, 1984) and then are regressed on measures of financial constraints. The results show that increasing financial pressure also has a positive impact on co-ops' technical efficiency growth.

Chapter 5 focuses on the role that financial constraints have in conditioning the self-employment choice of women from an ethnic background in England. The notion that the availability of external financial resources can affect adversely self-employment is quite established in the economic literature. Indeed, theoretical work has shown that both/either the lack of sufficient initial capital and/or insufficient access to credit markets work as binding constraints on individuals' choice between salaried employment and self-employment – a hypothesis supported by several empirical studies (Evans and Jovanovic (1989); Evans and Leighton (1989); Holtz-Eakin *et al.* (1994); Lindh and Ohlsson (1996, 1998); Blanchflower and Oswald (1998); Hamilton and Fox (1998)). So, the availability of collateral determines the cost of external funding and in this case, the larger the availability of personal assets the lower is the cost of external finance. Obviously this argument is stronger in the case of women from a minority background as they may have not have control over financial resources and lack the necessary connections and experience to overcome this problem. The implication is that women may be financially discriminated if they try to get external resources to fund their entrepreneurial activity. The evidence that is typically advanced to support this view is the small volume of loans to women-owned start-ups. However, it is possible to argue that this may be the result of either a small number of applications or the fact that women may have different preferences and that they may be more risk-averse than men. However, one problem is that this effect is very difficult to quantify as information on the intentions to set up a new company are needed. In this chapter I consider again these issues by testing empirically the extent to which the expectation of future finance constraints can deter potential borrowers from applying. The novelty of the analysis is that I focus on the start-up stage, unlike the previous literature that has tested the extent to which women-owned companies (that are already established) are financially constrained. More specifically, the purpose of this chapter is to analyse the relationship between finance constraints, gender and ethnic background and the individual's self-employment choice using English data drawn from the *Household Survey of Entrepreneurship*, 2003 (the Survey, henceforth) recently made available by the Small Business Support (SBS) Unit at the English Department of Trade and Industry (DTI). Empirically I use a variety of econometric methods to address these research questions: I first evaluate the extent to which finance constraints have an adverse impact on the probability of being self-employed and then whether these are compounded by gender and ethnic background. Therefore I will estimate a probit model where the self-employment choice is the dependent variable and measures of financial constraints, gender and ethnicity (and their interactions with the measures of financial constraints) appear among the regressors. In a second model, I will try to quantify the extent to which our two main variables of interest (gender and ethnicity) have an impact only on the probability that individuals have of experiencing financial constraints first, so that only those who do not have financial constraints can then become self-employed. This is an attempt to solve the eventual endogeneity problem that may affect the previous estimates as the probability of experiencing financial constraints may be endogenous. Econometrically, this is equivalent to estimating a two-stage Heckman model where in the first stage I model the probability of experiencing financial constraints as a function of gender and ethnic background, while in the second stage, I model the career choice of those that do not experience financial constraints as a function of variables like ability, human capital and so on. Finally, I will test whether gender and ethnicity affect mainly the access to external finance, while the self-employment choice is influenced by other factors (like entrepreneurial ability, current employment status and so on) that are independent of gender and ethnic background. Again this will be done by estimating a two-stage Heckman model where in the first stage the probability of accessing external funding is affected by both gender and ethnicity, while in the second stage I model the probability of individuals to become self-employed once they approached external funders as a function of their ability, education and so on. The results show that either gender or ethnic background does not appear to enhance the finance constraints that then have a negative impact on the self-employment choice. On the contrary, these are compounded by the lack of collateral and by the location. Also it seems that a self-selection mechanism is at work where women (from any ethnic background) expect to encounter substantial financial constraints (even if this may not necessarily be justified) and then decide not to seek external funds and so to set up a new company. Finally, Chapter 6 presents the main conclusions from the work and highlights new avenues for eventual future research.

A few lessons can be drawn from these three case-studies that are of general relevance. The first is the most obvious but as such it is sometimes forgotten: finance constraints generate additional effects beside that of increasing the cost of borrowing (and so reducing the investment expenditure and so on). Some of these effects can be beneficial, as shown in Chapter 3, and this must be taken into consideration when trying to compute the overall effects of finance constraints on economic outcomes. This argument obviously does not imply that financial constraints may necessarily be a "blessing in disguise". Indeed, it is well known that there are more negative direct effects of financial constraints that may have the potential effect of slowing down economic growth and make the economy more vulnerable to negative productivity shocks. What I argue is that up to a certain point, the financial constraints can have some positive impact that can attenuate (even if not totally counterbalance) the negative effect. For example, a firm that is technically inefficient may benefit from a tightening of financial constraints but this does not mean that the extra resources generated by the reduction in inefficiency may be enough to counterbalance the negative impact of financial constraints, like the reduced rate of innovation. Also, this result suggests that keeping some organizational slack in the firm may make sense if the firm operates in an industry that is frequently subject to negative shocks that can be followed by credit crunches and so on. Second, it is clear that increasing financial pressure may complement other forces (like increasing product market competition) to improve firms' performance when there is a clear link between performance and workers' participation. However, these considerations drive another question: what is the impact of financial constraints on firms that for some reasons have no organizational slack? In the terminology adopted in the book this is equivalent to asking what happens to firms that are on the frontier when the financial pressure increases. Even if it is not explicitly modelled in the following chapters, there is a potential non-linearity in the relationship between technical efficiency and financial constraints. Indeed, firms on the frontier that are exposed to intense financial pressure may need to reduce their activities in order to cope with the worsening of the financial pressure. A final important lesson from these case studies is that economic agents tend to internalize the possibility that they can encounter financial constraints and this may affect in a rather powerful fashion their consequent behaviour. The relationship between gender, finance constraints and self-employment is rather eloquent in this respect. Indeed, women may perceive they will be financially constrained even if this may not be entirely justified and give up altogether the prospect of setting up their own company. So for the policy-maker it is important to be able to influence the perception of the prospective finance constraints firms and consumers may face in addition to trying to relax the credit constraints altogether.

2 Credit constraints and economic outcomes

A short survey

2.1 Introduction

The last 30 years have witnessed a dramatic revival of the academic research on the asymmetric distribution of information among borrowers and lenders and its impact on the properties of the competitive equilibrium in the credit market.[1] This interest has been prompted by the research of Stiglitz and Weiss (1981, 1985, 1987) first, and Williamson (1986, 1987a, 1987b) afterwards, who have extended to the study of the credit market the formal apparatus devised by Akerlof (1970) to analyse trade under imperfect information. While their models focus on different informational problems,[2] they both conclude that the resulting competitive equilibrium is inefficient as some potential borrowers (who are still willing to borrow at the equilibrium interest rate) will not get credit in equilibrium as lenders are not willing to lend to them. The argument behind this result is well known. Both in the case of adverse selection and of moral hazard, banks may wish to hold the interest rate below the market clearing level since an increase of the interest rate on loans may adversely affect the rate of return to banks (as riskier applicants may now have the incentive to join the pool of applicants). Therefore, financial institutions cannot use the interest rate as a variable that allows either to sort borrowers according to their riskiness or as an incentive mechanism; so at the end they have to resort to credit rationing to avoid potential future losses. Thus some borrowers will be rationed in equilibrium with the result that they will not get the necessary financial resources to carry out their productive activities.

Afterwards, a substantial empirical literature has analysed the implications of the financial constraints due to informational imperfections on both firms' productive activities and business formation, among the many possible activities.[3] As it has been pointed out by Nickell and Nicolitsas (1999), the main impact of credit rationing is that of increasing the cost of borrowing for both firms and consumers and this of course has a direct, adverse impact on both the investment activity and the formation of new firms. Indeed, the theoretical models on credit rationing entail a clear prediction on the characteristics of the economic agents that are likely to be rationed in equilibrium: typically, young and small firms may be constrained in their access to external financial resources as lenders may consider young age (and so lack of track record) and small size as signals of the inexperience of these potential borrowers and so of the riskiness of the invest-ment projects proposed by them (Fazzari *et al.*, 1988; Hubbard and Kashyap, 1992; Schaller, 1993; Gilchrist and Himmelberg, 1995; Hubbard *et al.*, 1995). Equally, potential lenders may be reluctant to support financially the creation of new firms as it is difficult for them to assess the future market prospects of these new companies and therefore their relative riskiness (Evans and Jovanovic, 1982; Goldberg and White, 1998). In both cases, credit rationing creates the con-ditions for the emergence of a link between the firms' productive activities (say demand for investments, firm's growth and new business formation) and the firm's (or the individual's in the case of the formation of new firms) retained earnings (or personal wealth in the case of individuals). Therefore, a rationed firm's demand for investment will depend positively on its balance sheet position as a strengthened balance sheet implies a borrower has more internal resources to use either directly to fund the project or as additional collateral to obtain external funds (Gertler *et al.*, 1991; Gertler and Gilchrist, 1994; Chirinko and Schaller, 1995). This last hypothesis (i.e. the positive relationship between the demand for investments and the firm's balance sheet position) has been extensively tested and the empirical findings tend to support it generally.[4] Equally, the formation of new business will be affected by the availability of personal financial resources of the potential new entrepreneurs. Indeed, when there are credit constraints, external financing may be unavailable or insufficient for the set-up of a new company and this creates a link between the wealth of the potential entrepreneur and the decision to start a business as wealthier individuals will be more likely to start a new company (Curran and Blackburn, 1993; Cosh and Hughes, 2003; Fraser, 2005). In this context, financial constraints will cause the supply and the demand for credit to be related to the personal characteristics of the borrower; for instance, the borrower's creditworthiness will be judged against some criteria that take into account the personal financial history of the applicant. So, for instance, it is often argued that women from a minority background are discrimi-nated against in credit markets and this view is usually supported by the objec-tively small number of companies run by women from a minority background who rely on loans to fund their productive activities. Now, this argument is based on the assumption that lenders reject loans applications from female applicants "ceteris paribus" because they use their personal characteristics – like lack of collateral (as women do not tend to have control over economic resources), limited education and the unpaid reproductive responsibilities (Goffee and Scase, 1983; Aldrich, 1989) – as variables that allow to predict the economic prospects of the new company, in spite of the fact that all these features may not necessar-ily affect the future company's profitability.

In this chapter I will present a selective review of the most relevant academic research that looks at the credit rationing and at the impact of credit constraints on both firms' demand for investment and the formation of new companies. The objective here is not to provide a comprehensive review of the relevant literature in these areas but to highlight the key issues which have emerged from previous studies. These will provide the basis for the inclusion of specific variables in the models estimated in the remaining chapters in the book and also shape the discussion of the results. The chapter is divided into two parts: in the first one, I will describe the theoretical literature dealing mainly with the allocative consequences of informational asymmetries in the credit market at the micro level; more specifically I will describe in some detail the seminal papers of Stiglitz and Weiss (1981) on the effects of adverse selection and of Williamson (1986) focusing on the moral hazard with costly monitoring. This will then be followed by the analysis of the more "modern" literature in this field that wants to identify the conditions under which the optimal properties of the competitive equilibrium can be restored in the presence of asymmetric information. Also, I will introduce the main empirical studies examining the impact of credit constraints on firms' investment demand. In the second part of the chapter I will review the literature on self-employment, financial constraints and gender. More specifically, I will start by considering the literature on self-employment and entrepreneurship that focuses on the motives behind the individuals' choice of becoming self-employed. Afterwards, I focus on the literature that analyses more specifically the relationship between entrepreneurship, financial constraints and gender.

The structure of the chapter is therefore the following. Section 2.2 introduces briefly the main models of credit rationing as proposed by Stiglitz and Weiss, first, and Williamson, afterwards. This is followed by an analysis of the models that considers the conditions under which the optimality of the competitive equilibrium in the credit market can be restored. The implications of credit constraints on the firms' demand for investment are discussed in Section 2.2. The literature of self-employment choice, gender and financial constraints is presented in Section 2.3. Finally, some concluding remarks on this literature are offered in Section 2.4.

2.2 Asymmetric information in the credit market and its impact on firms' demand for investment: a brief survey

The purpose of this section is to present briefly the main results of the literature dealing with the consequences of the asymmetric distribution of information on the credit market equilibrium and its subsequent effects on firms' demand for investment.

2.2.1 Allocative effects of the informational problems in the credit market

Many of the ideas in this literature can be best understood in the context of the Akerlof's (1970) paper on the "lemons" problem. This paper famously illustrates how asymmetric information between buyers and sellers about the quality of a product can cause a market to malfunction. The argument runs as follows: the market price reflects the buyers' perceptions of the average quality of the product being sold and because of this, sellers of low-quality goods tend to receive a premium at the expense of those selling high-quality goods. This distortion in turn may affect the level of market activity; indeed, low-quality sellers have the incentive to enter the market so to take advantage of this premium and so the average quality of goods sold out in this market may tend to decrease over time so much so that some high-quality sellers will prefer to stay out of the market altogether. In the worst scenario, this mechanism may even preclude the market from opening. The literature on credit market inefficiencies applies Akerlof's basic ideas to the working of the credit market. In a very influential paper, Stiglitz and Weiss (1981) exploit informational asymmetries to explain the type of credit rationing happening when the market denies funds to loan applicants with characteristics identical to those receiving loans. The authors assume that the potential borrowers' projects differ in terms of riskiness unobserved to the bank (adverse selection). It is also assumed that banks issue standard debt contracts that pay lenders a fixed interest rate if the project yield is sufficiently high, and pays the net yield otherwise. Thus, for a given loan rate, lenders earn a lower than expected return on loans to low-quality borrowers (in other words, borrowers with riskier projects). This occurs because an unobserved mean-preserving spread in a borrower's project return distribution reduces the expected payment to lenders under default. Also, Stiglitz and Weiss show that, given their assumptions, the loan supply curve may bend backwards and that credit rationing can emerge as a consequence due to the fact that the loan demand and supply curve may not intersect. A rise in the interest rate lowers the average borrower quality as those with relatively safe projects are the first to drop out. Thus, further increases in the interest rate may lower the lenders' expected return making the loan supply curve bend backwards. The quantity of loans offered is the maximum the supply curve permits. The excess demand for loans persists because adjustment in the interest rate cannot equilibrate the market as further increases of the interest rates only lower the supply of loans offered.

Other papers explore the impact of moral hazard on the credit market equilibrium. Moral hazard is another form by which asymmetric information can manifest itself in the credit market. Borrowers can affect the result of an investment project in several ways: for instance, the successful outcome of a project may be dependent on the amount of effort the borrower devotes to it. Alternatively, a borrower may choose a riskier project from a set of potential projects. Williamson in 1986 (and then 1987a and 1987b) analyses the circumstances under which moral hazard with costly monitoring can generate credit rationing. He considers the problem of a lender and a borrower interested in formulating a bilateral loan agreement. The two key assumptions in his model are that the lender must pay a fixed cost to observe the returns to the borrower's project (i.e. the verification of the state is costly – so-called costly state verification) and second, the borrower does not have sufficient collateral to fully secure the loan. The dilemma the lender faces is the following: he is aware that the borrower if unmonitored has the incentive to misreport the project outcome but he also knows that it is inefficient to commit to auditing the borrower under all circumstances. In this setting, rationing may occur because the expected default costs (stemming from the fact that verifying the outcome of the project is costly) may make it prohibitively expensive for borrowers to obtain funds from lenders with higher opportunity costs.

2.2.2 Asymmetric information, credit market and collateral

Afterwards, many papers (Bester, 1985; Hellwig, 1986; De Meza and Webb, 1987; Besanko and Thakor, 1987) have elaborated on these themes with their results often depending greatly on the particular type of informational asymmetries posed between borrowers and lenders. A common conclusion has emerged from these early studies: informational asymmetries create an incentive problem inducing banks to ration credit. Not surprisingly, some research has been conducted to clarify the conditions under which the optimal properties of the credit market can be restored also in the presence of asymmetric information. Indeed, the results obtained in the Stiglitz and Weiss' papers can be easily criticized by recalling that banks' contracts are usually conditional not only on the interest rate, but also on collateral requirements, loan size and so on. Therefore it is possible to argue that while banks do not want to raise the interest rate to avoid the adverse effects of these increases on the average profitability of their pool of applicants, they can still use other features of the contract to screen applicants. Bester (1984, 1987) was the first to formalize this argument and in a couple of papers he showed that in a credit market where banks cannot know a priori the riskiness of the borrowers (i.e. the credit market is affected by adverse selection), collateral can be used as a useful screening device that can help to solve the credit rationing problem. However, it has been shown that collateral can be used as a screening device as long as the potential applicants are endowed with sufficient personal wealth that can be used to fully guarantee the loan. The possibility of obtaining a separating equilibrium when applicants do not own sufficient personal wealth has been examined by both Besanko and Thakor (1987) and Schmidt-Mohr (1997). Indeed, on these occurrences, Besanko and Thakor (1987) have suggested that the size of the loan can be used together with the collateral and the interest rate to screen the potential borrowers. In this case, good-quality entrepreneurs may be forced to accept larger loans than required to signal the fact that they are good-quality borrowers and therefore a separating equilibrium can still be obtained. Schmidt-Mohr (1997) has showed that the size of the loan an entrepreneur is willing to accept may serve as a signalling device of the riskiness of the project and so it can be used as an alternative to collateral as long as the borrowers have different degrees of risk aversion.

Also in the case of moral hazard, collateral can be used as an incentive device to influence the entrepreneur's choice of effort. Early models have analysed the conditions under which a separating equilibrium is still possible in the presence of moral hazard. Boot *et al.* (1991) show how to use the two main elements of a contract (interest rate and collateral requirements) to reduce the default's probability. They have built a model where the probability of success of the investment project is influenced by the effort the entrepreneur puts in the project. The economic environment is the usual one: one borrower has to seek external finance to fund a project that can be either successful or not. The success probability depends on two parameters: the quality of the project (varying itself across borrowers) and a set of actions that can be taken by the borrower once the loan has been granted (moral hazard). None of the two parameters can be observed by the bank: the quality of the project is known only to the borrower while the choice of the action can only be observed ex post by the bank. It is assumed that the borrower's quality and the choice of the action are (partial) substitutes. Indeed, for the borrower the choice of the action is costly and it is costlier to choose the good action rather than to choose the bad action. In addition, it is assumed that the marginal returns of a good action are decreasing in the quality of the borrowers and therefore, a good borrower will be less likely to choose a good action than a bad borrower. The loan contract is made of two elements: the interest rate and the collateral requirements. The borrower's action is chosen after receiving a contract from the bank. Now, if the borrower could pledge sufficient collateral to make the loan riskless, then the moral hazard problem would be resolved. On the contrary, it is assumed that the borrower can never post enough collateral as the bank always evaluates the collateral as a fraction of what it is worth to the borrower. As effort decreases the probability of default, then the incentive effects of the interest rate and collateral are opposite: collateral induces the entrepreneur to put more effort so as to minimize the default's probability, while high interest rates mean that part of the surplus produced by the borrower will be appropriated by the bank and so the borrower will have less incentive to increase the effort and ensure a successful outcome of the project.

A common assumption of the models reviewed so far is that there exists perfect competition in the loan market and that therefore the zero-profit condition on the credit market needs to be imposed. The behaviour of a bank in a monopolistic loan market when there is adverse selection has been analysed by Besanko and Thakor (1987). In their model, the authors consider a loan market where the bank acts as a price-setting monopolist. There are two types of borrowers, low risk and high risk. Each investor has a given endowment that can be either safely invested in a deposit or invested in a risky project that yields a given return if successful or zero otherwise. The bank does not know whether the single applicant is high or low risk; it only knows the fraction of borrowers that is high risk (and consequently the fraction of applicants that is low risk). Under full information, the bank never requires a borrower to secure a loan with collateral because collateral is costly to liquidate in case of default. Indeed, under full information, the bank can specify an interest rate equal to the return in the successful state less the imputed cost of undertaking the risky project and this would be enough for the bank to ensure itself against the high-risk borrowers. Obviously, low-risk borrowers would pay a higher interest rate than high-risk borrowers as in this case the bank wants to extract all the borrowers' surplus. In the presence of adverse selection, if the expected social surplus for a high-risk borrower is sufficiently large, both types receive a loan at the interest rate the high-risk borrower will be charged in the case of full information. The main feature of this optimal contract is that the collateral pledged by each borrower is zero. Therefore, collateral is not an optimal sorting device in this environment: if the bank simultaneously raises the collateral and lowers the interest rate offered to high-risk borrowers, the low types would have even more of an incentive to choose the high-risk contract instead of the low-risk contract. The low-risk borrowers really prefer the lower interest rate but are not as concerned about the higher collateral requirements because they know that their probability of failure is low.

If the credit market is perfectly competitive, then there is an excess supply of entrepreneurs while typically the number of potential borrowers is limited. This implies that all the rents will be appropriated by the entrepreneurs and this will make it difficult to stop borrowers from undertaking riskier projects. However a simple way to solve this problem is by introducing an additional agent who is not the residual claimant of the rents and therefore does not have the interest in undertaking unprofitable projects. An example of this type of agent may be the manager of the firm. Acemoglu (1997) models a market with both adverse selection and moral hazard and shows that the resulting equilibrium is not inefficient when entrepreneurs can hire a manager (who has the same preferences as the owner of the firm) to run their projects. More precisely, when control is delegated to the manager, this agent will not consider unprofitable projects.

The adverse effects of both adverse selection and moral hazard could be reduced if the financial intermediaries and the borrowers could enter into repeated interactions (Gertler, 1992; Boot and Thakor, 1994; Beaudry and Poitevin, 1995). For instance, Boot and Thakor (1994) consider a multi-period setting where lenders and borrowers can renegotiate their contract over time. The model shows that in the initial round (as the bank does not know the quality of the applicant) it is optimal for the bank to charge a high interest rate and have high collateral requirements. However, the bank has got the incentive to design a contract where the borrower can have a contract with a low interest rate and no collateral requirements in later periods conditional on the successful repayment in the first period. Beaudry and Poitevin (1995) examine the case in which borrowers are allowed to contract loans and reveal information at different stages before the project terminates. In this case, a separating equilibrium cannot be achieved in the first stage even when wealth availability is not a binding constraint. This happens as risky firms know they can always re-contract at later stages and diversify their risk if they reveal their type. So the possibility of re-contracting may be welfare-improving. When re-contracting is allowed, a pooling equilibrium occurs in the first stage and both types diversify perfectly at later stages. Also, reputation effects may mitigate asymmetric information problems in credit markets over time. One method of sustaining reputation effects is by restricting a lender's access to a borrower's credit history via credit bureau policy (Vercammen, 1995).

Finally, most models of credit rationing assume that either adverse selection or moral hazard is present. However, when both adverse selection and moral hazard are present Vercammen (2002) shows that the efficient properties of the equilibrium can be restored. Indeed, adverse selection will be welfare improving in a pooling equilibrium if (a) the direct welfare loss from the adverse selection is not excessively large, and (b) the negative moral hazard effects are smaller with adverse selection than without it. This result is based on the cross-subsidization that occurs in the pooling equilibrium due to adverse selection. Specifically, the moral hazard causes borrowers to supply an inefficiently low level of effort and the distortion is worse the higher the interest rate. In an adverse selection pooling equilibrium, the low-quality borrower is charged a comparatively lower interest rate while the high-quality borrower is charged a comparatively higher interest rate. Because low-quality borrowers are more severely affected by moral hazard than high-quality borrowers, this cross-subsidization results in a higher overall level of effort and thus a lower average probability of default across all borrowers. These efficiency gains can more than offset the welfare loss due to the impact of adverse selection on the borrowers' choice of investment.

2.2.3 Credit constraints and firms' investment demand: the empirical studies

Credit market rationing can have relevant effects on firms' capital accumulation as it can reduce the efficiency of the investment process, inducing, in the worst cases, an investment collapse. Indeed, firms might not be able to fund their planned investments as they do not have access to sufficient external resources. If so, an immediate testable implication of these models of credit rationing is that for a debt-constrained firm, the investment demand depends positively on their balance sheet positions. Indeed, large retained earnings imply that the firms have more resources available to use directly to fund their project; this reduces the borrowers' cost of obtaining external funds by lowering the informational risk that outside lenders bear and in turn stimulates investment. Such a prediction has been tested by checking the significance of cash-flow variables into either models of demand for investments or production functions.

Many empirical studies, using different specifications of the investment demand and different data-sets, have shown the failure of the perfect capital market hypothesis for firms selected a priori to be more likely to face capital market frictions (Blanchard et al., 1993; Hubbard, 1995). The approach tests the null hypothesis of a correctly specified investment model by testing the significance of liquidity variables and uses their pattern across firms to suggest the importance of finance constraints for these firms. In their pathbreaking study, Fazzari et al. (1988) tested for the significance of cash-flow variables on the demand for investment using three models of the demand for investment the accelerator model, the Jorgenson model (1970) and the Tobin's q model (Poterba and Summers, 1983; Schiantarelli and Georgoutsos, 1990; Schaller, 1990; Chirinko, 1993)[5] using a panel of 49 firms over the period 1969–1984 drawn

Table 2.1 Finance constraints and the demand for investments: the Tobin's q

Author	Country	Data format	Period	Source
Fazzari	USA	Panel	1969–1984	Value Line Data Base Corporate Database
Hoshi	Giappone	Panel	1965–1986	Nikkei Financial Data Tapes
Schaller	Canada	Panel	1973–1986	Laval Database and Financial Post Annual Corporate Database

from the Value Line data base. Firms were sorted by retention ratios under the hypothesis that firms retaining a higher percentage of their equity income must face higher costs for external funds. Therefore cash-flow variables should be significant for high-retention firms rather than for low-retention and unconstrained firms. The main result is that, overall, investment is significantly more sensitive to current cash flow for firms with a high retention ratio than a frictionless neoclassical model would predict. Also, the conclusions are more dramatic for new and small firms. These findings are largely confirmed by data from different countries and different tippes of firms (Fazzari *et al.*, 1988; Gertler and Hubbard, 1988; Hayashi and Inoue, 1991; Devereux and Schiantarelli, 1990; Hoshi *et al.*, 1992) (see Table 2.1 for a summary of the main features of these and other works).

A second set of studies has taken a similar approach but has examined the finance constraints hypothesis using the Euler equation (Schiantarelli, 1996) supplemented with a borrowing constraint (see, among others, Gertler and Kashyap, 1991; Whited, 1991, 1992; Bond and Meghir, 1994; Hubbard *et al.*, 1995; see Table 2.2 for a summary of these and other works). When this constraint is binding, the associated multiplier enters the error term. This implication can then be evaluated by the correlation between the instruments and residuals in the over-identified model (Wu, 1973, 1974). Firms believed a priori to be constrained in financial markets tend to fail these specification tests while the remaining firms tend to pass. Further, to highlight the alternative hypothesis the multiplier is parameterized in terms of variables representing finance constraints. Gertler *et al.* (1991) have measured this variable by the spreads between the interest rates on assets with the same maturity but different degrees of riskiness to capture the relationship between monetary policies and credit availability. Whited (1992), on the contrary, has specified the shadow cost by employing variables like the ratio between the long-run debt and the firm's market value. Kwon (2000) has taken a different approach and has estimated the impact of credit constraints on the demand for productive factors (fixed investment and employment) (Pindyck and Rotemberg, 1983), and unlike the previous research papers in the area he has examined data in the service sector (namely retail firms). Not surprisingly, he finds strong evidence for the impact of financial constraints on the demand for factors. Also the estimates show that financial factors may magnify swings in input demands of firms subject to credit constraints through the impact of finance constraints on the discount rates.

Table 2.2 Finance constraints and the demand for investments: Euler equation

Author	Country	Data format	Period	Source
Whited	USA	Panel	1976–1991	Standard and Poor's COMPUSTAT
Hubbard	USA	Panel	1976–1987	Standard and Poor's COMPUSTAT
Ng and Schaller	Canada	Panel	1973–1986	Laval Database and Financial Post Annual Corporate Database
Kwon	USA	Panel	1977–1991	Citicorp

The small literature analysing the impact of finance constraints on firms' productivity has produced interesting and intriguing results. For instance, Nickell and Nicolitsas (1999) have investigated the impact on company behaviour of increases in financial pressure using a data-set of UK companies. Their results show that (as expected) demand for investment decreases when the cost of external funding increases. More interestingly, they also find that the adverse financial shock reduces the firm's working capital and obviously this has a direct negative impact on employment (even after controlling for current and expected wages). Also, the negative shock has a negative impact on pay rises while interestingly enough, increasing financial pressure has a small positive effect on total factor productivity. One explanation for this is that workers may be willing to accept a reduction in wages to offset the negative impact of financial constraints and this, jointly with the fact that managers are risk-averse, may explain the positive impact of financial pressure on productivity. A related line of research has considered the relationship between the state of competition in the product market and the financial pressure. Now, from a theoretical standpoint, it can be proved that these two mechanisms are complementary in the sense that firms with a higher debt-repayment obligation will try to improve their performance (both in terms of productivity growth and productivity in levels) if the competitive pressure is increasing as long as the managers' preferences are for a high level of slack in the firm. However, the empirical evidence on this point is rather ambiguous. Nickell *et al.* (1997) have analysed the joint impact of financial pressure and product market competition on productivity growth using a data-set of British firms; their results indicate that for these firms, as financial pressure increases the positive impact of competition on productivity growth decreases. In other words they work as substitutes. Afterwards, Aghion *et al.* (2003) have focused on the innovation and has looked at the interaction between financial pressure and competition in a data-set of British firms listed on the London Stock Exchange Market: they identify the firms facing the highest financial pressure and consider whether the impact of competition differs for them relative to the whole sample of firms. Their results tend to be inconclusive in the sense that financial pressure and competition appear to have no relationship on the firms' productivity.

2.3 Self-employment choice, gender and financial constraints

2.3.1 Introduction

It is a well-known fact that the number of firms that are owned by women has increased substantially over the last decade (Brush and Hisrich, 1991; Arenius and Autio, 2006). For instance, data relative to 2000 show that 40 per cent of all US companies are owned by women (see, for instance, the data contained by Merrett and Gruidl, 2000; Renzulli *et al.*, 2000). Europe as well can boast a comparable increase in the number of firms that are women-owned (Carter *et al.*, 2001). For example, in the Netherlands, 34 per cent of self-employed individuals are women while in Finland, Denmark, Spain, Belgium and the UK the percentage is somewhat lower, with figures of around 25 per cent (Duchenaut, 1997; Nilsson, 1997). Not surprisingly, the economic research devoted to the analysis of female entrepreneurship has followed suit and now a substantial literature is available that allows us to understand the main issues related to female entrepreneurship (see reviews in Gatewood *et al.*, 2003; Carter *et al.*, 2004; Bruni *et al.*, 2005). Naturally the majority of early studies on women business owners has focused on North America (e.g. Hisrich and Brush, 1986; Riding and Swift, 1990; Fabowale *et al.*, 1995; Haines *et al.*, 1999; Haynes and Haynes, 1999; Coleman, 2000); however, by now there exists a substantial part of the empirical literature that focuses on European countries.

An obvious starting point for any survey on female entrepreneurship is the literature on self-employment and entrepreneurship that focuses on the motives behind the individuals' choice of becoming self-employed. This literature shares a common starting point that is the career choice model where an economic agent chooses self-employment as its future career if the expected utility of doing so exceeds the expected utility of salaried employment. This model provides a first motivation for self-employment: indeed, the higher the earnings differential between self-employment and salaried employment, the more likely individuals are to become entrepreneurs (e.g. Rees and Shah, 1986; Fujii and Hawley, 1991; Taylor, 1996).[6] In other words, the lower the expected salaried income the higher the probability an individual has of becoming self-employed. Indeed, Evans and Leighton (1989) find that those who switch from salaried work to self-employment are individuals whose expected wage is not high due to either low education or long unemployment spells. Also Taylor (1996), using British data, finds that an individual is more likely to be self-employed if the unemployment rate in the region where he resides is rather high. Later research has started to analyse the importance of other (less tangible) factors in the choice between salaried employment and self-employment. In Hamilton (2000), for instance, much of the earnings differential between salaried and self-employment is due to the relatively large non-pecuniary benefits derived from the latter, like independence and job satisfaction. Not surprisingly, Blanchflower and Oswald (1998) and Blanchflower (2000) report that self-employed individuals report higher levels of job and life satisfaction. Also, Taylor (1996) found that the independence offered by self-employment is a factor that affects positively the individual's probability of self-employment.

A significant portion of the literature on entrepreneurship has focused on the extent to which access to financial resources can affect the entrepreneurial choice (Evans and Jovanovic (1989); Evans and Leigthon (1989); Holtz-Eakin *et al.* (1994); Winker (1999)). Theoretical work has indeed shown that both/either the lack of sufficient initial capital and/or insufficient access to credit markets work as binding constraints on individuals' choice between salaried employment and self-employment – a hypothesis supported by several empirical studies. For example, Evans and Jovanovic (1989) and Evans and Leighton (1989) find that the probability of an individual being self-employed increases with the individual's net worth in US data. Similarly, Holtz-Eakin *et al.* (1994) and Blanchflower and Oswald (1998), by using US and British data respectively, find that inheritances and family gifts increase the probability of self-employment. Also, Lindh and Ohlsson (1996) find that in Sweden the probability of self-employment is higher for those who receive lottery windfall gains. Lindh and Ohlsson (1998) take the issue of credit constraints a step further and look at how the degree of wealth inequality in an economy can affect the aggregate proportion of self-employed workers. However, financial constraints may affect the individual's probability of becoming self-employed in different ways. For instance, they can affect the individual's accumulation of human capital that in turn may also affect self-employment income through its impact on the skills of the self-employed. However, it may also have an indirect effect in that more skilled and able individuals are likely to find it easier to raise external finance (such as equity and loans) to become self-employed (Chandler and Hanks, 1998). In fact, Cressy and Toivanen (2001) have argued that this indirect effect totally explains access to finance and therefore, it is human capital and not finance that acts as the main constraint on the self-employment choice.

There is a part of the literature on self-employment that has analysed how the self-employment choice may be dependent on whether the parents are self-employed themselves (see Dunn and Holtz-Eakin, 2000; Taylor, 1996; Hout and Rosen, 2000). In this literature, the assumption is that entrepreneurial ability can be transferred from one generation to the other and that therefore the parental labour market status may be important in facilitating this intergenerational transfer. Dunn and Holtz-Eakin (2000) find that having a self-employed parent has a strong positive effect on the probability of men's self-employment. Interestingly, though, this is true for men but not for women where this effect is not particularly strong. Similarly, Hout and Rosen (2000) confirm that whether or not the father is self-employed may explain the offspring's self-employment choice.

Some authors have tried to analyse whether discrimination on formal labour markets may explain the individual's choice for self-employment. This issue has been examined mostly with reference to ethnic minorities. Bates (1991) has tested whether the typically small size of loans received by firms whose owners are from a minority background (once they are compared to white-owned firms) could be attributed to credit discrimination. Fairlie and Meyer (1996) find that, while ethnicity and race are important determinants of self-employment, the individual's decision process for the self-employment choice is very similar across racial and ethnic groups; in other words, discrimination does not affect the self-employment choice. Borjas and Bronars (1989) explain observed ethnic differences in US self-employment on the basis of consumer discrimination, but they cannot find evidence of the impact of discrimination on self-employment. Finally some research has looked at the possible impact of different government policy measures on self-employment. Bruce (2000) has analysed the differential tax treatment of salaried employment and self-employment and has argued that self-employment is relatively more attractive than salaried employment because of the structure of taxation on self-employment income. Also, Fan and White (2003) find that individuals who live in US states with higher personal bankruptcy exemptions are much more likely to be self-employed as the exemption acts as insurance.

These studies focus exclusively on the self-employment decision without considering gender issues directly. However, it is important to recall that gender-related factors are quite important to explain the self-employment choice as labour market participation and labour opportunities vary considerably between men and women (OECD, 1998). Not surprisingly, some research has considered the nature of the constraints women face when they decide to go for self-employment and the impact they can have on the self-employment choice itself. The general perception of the literature on self-employment and gender is that for women, starting-up a business is more difficult (Carter and Cannon, 1992; Carter and Rosa, 1998; Carter *et al.*, 2001) and also that these difficulties do not disappear as the company grows (Johnson and Storey, 1993; Warren-Smith and Jackson, 2004). This literature will be analysed in the next sub-section.

2.3.2 Self-employment choice, gender and financial constraints

Traditionally, literature on the motives behind female self-employment has emphasized the fact that women may view self-employment as a closer substitute for either part-time employment or being out of the labour force. Indeed, women at the lower end of the skill distribution may also have different occupational strategies from men and may desire non-standard work schedules because of family responsibilities (Darian, 1975; Casper and O'Connell, 1998; Presser, 1995; Bianchi, 2000). In this view, then, self-employment can therefore be a more viable option for a woman than salaried employment as it can reduce the cost of child care and offers time flexibility (Connelly, 1992). Not surprisingly, Connelly (1992) finds that the choice between self-employment and salaried self-employment is conditioned by the presence of young children. However, this view has changed over time. Indeed, a recent study by Lombard (2001) finds that most of the rise in female self-employment is due to the women's increased earnings potential in self-employment (Devine, 1994). Along similar lines, Wellington (2006) examines the hypothesis that educated, married women may decide to be self-employed to balance the family demands and the career's needs. The findings suggest that married women prefer self-employment and this effect is stronger for more educated women. However, there is not a strong support for the hypothesis that the increase in self-employment has been driven by the need to respond to the demand of family care.

As for the finance of female-led business, although there is a growing body of literature addressing the financing of women-owned businesses, not enough is known about the attempts of women-led start-ups to access bank loans and their success in securing those loans (Fabowale *et al.*, 1995). As for all small businesses (Meyer, 1998), bank lending is the most important overall source of external funding and also for women-led start-ups (Hamilton and Fox, 1998; Kotey, 1999; Jones, 2001; Howorth, 2001; Berger and Udell, 2002a). Research in this area suggests that gender has a direct impact on the type of finance used in the sense that female entrepreneurs finance their businesses differently from men[7] (Apilado and Millington, 1992). Rosa *et al.* (1994) and Verheul and Thurik (2001) found that women tend to start out with less initial capital.[8] Women-owned businesses are often self-financed – women are less likely to go into debt – and they launch businesses with less money than men do (Belcourt *et al.*, 1991; Coleman, 2000). The dominant sources of funding used by women-owned businesses are earnings from the company, savings, home equity loans, credit cards and family loans. When they do secure debt funding, it is most often from savings and loans from family members (Schwartz, 1979; Coleman, 2000). Also women-owned companies are significantly less likely to use bank loans than men to finance their business (Coleman and Carsky, 1996). It has been argued that securing loans from banks is difficult for women-owned businesses (Van Auken *et al.*, 1993; Chaganti *et al.*, 1995, Orser *et al.*, 2000). Uzzi (1999) found that women-owned businesses were less likely to apply for bank loans. Riding and Swift (1990) and Coleman (2000) have argued that this is the case because the terms under which women typically obtain credit are less favourable than those given to men. However, the empirical evidence does not always support these hypotheses. A US-based study by Treichel and Scott (2006) has examined women-owned businesses' experience with commercial bank credit by first considering the likelihood of applying for bank loans and then the outcome of the most recent loan by evaluating the likelihood that the loan application at banks was turned down. Finally, it tried to gauge the effect of gender on loan terms for successful applications. The results suggest that even after controlling for important business characteristics, women-owned businesses are significantly less likely to apply for a bank loan. Cavalluzzo *et al.* (2002) found no difference in the application experience of women-owned businesses after controlling for credit history, assets, sales and years in business. These results were corroborated by the 1998 Survey of Small Business Finance by Robb and Wolken (2002). The Annual Survey of Small Business (ASBS) for 2004, for example, suggests that obtaining finance was an obstacle for 15.5 per cent of all small firms and for 16.2 per cent of female-led enterprises.[9] The UK Survey of

SME Finances (UKSMEF) emphasizes another gender related issue, noting that "female-owned businesses pay significantly *higher* margins on term loans than male-owned businesses (2.9 versus 1.9 percentage points over Base)" (p. 18). However, empirical evidence for other European countries suggests that gender appears to make little difference to the choice of finance source utilized (Irwin and Scott, 2006). Finally, in a study by Arenius and Autio (2006), women and men business owners were equally likely to use external financing, refuting the results of Cole and Wolken (1995), Coleman and Carsky (1996, 1997), Haynes and Haynes (1999) and Coleman (2000).

How can these contrasting findings be reconciled? Three potential explanations have been put forward. First, it is possible that women-owned firms may face discrimination in securing loans from banks (Schwartz, 1979; Buttner and Rosen, 1989, 1992; Riding and Swift, 1990; Fabowale *et al.*, 1995; Haines *et al.*, 1999; Coleman, 2000; Orser *et al.*, 2000). However, it well may be that women are not actively discriminated but they simply do not seek external finance. Indeed, the belief that such discrimination exists may prevent women-owned businesses from applying for loans (Coleman, 2000) and may limit the size of the loan applied for by women-owned businesses (compared to the size of the loan applied for by businesses owned by men). Finally, it is possible that female- and men-led firms have different characteristics and this may explain the different financing patterns. What is the evidence in favour of each of these explanations?

Both objective and subjective evidence of discrimination has been found. Women-owned businesses were found to pay higher interest rates and had higher collateral requirements than businesses owned by men (Riding and Swift, 1990; Coleman, 2000), and also were given larger counter offers than those given to men (Buttner and Rosen, 1989). Scott (1986) finds that 44 out of 154 women believed that it would be easier for them to borrow money if they were men.[10] Also business women have indicated that they have difficulties in raising funds for their business using credit (Hisrich and O'Brien, 1982; Hisrich and Brush, 1984) and they experience a higher incidence of unmet credit needs (i.e. turned down on their most recent loan or did not apply for fear of being turned down) (Cavalluzzo *et al.*, 2002) and reported less satisfaction with lending terms than men as well (Orser *et al.*, 1994; Fabowale *et al.*, 1995). A study from Ireland aimed at understanding the women's perception of the experience of raising finance for their businesses found that overall, respondents had negative perceptions of banks as sources of finance – even those who had not actually approached them. Fay and Williams (1993) found that even after controlling for differences in the individual's net worth and past experience between men and women applicants, loan officers were less likely to offer loans to women because the women were deemed to have not sufficient collateral to use against the higher risk that a woman owned company is deemed to pose to a financial institution.

Some researchers have investigated the possible gender bias in banking lending practices (Strahan and Weston, 1998). Ennew and McKechnie (1998), for example, suggest that lenders may discriminate unconsciously. Some studies have selected a sample of women business owners and a corresponding sample of men business owners, and compared their experiences (Riding and Swift, 1990; Fabowale *et al.*, 1995). Other studies have tested the belief that women entrepreneurs are seen or treated differently in a lending decision (Buttner and Rosen, 1989; Fay and Williams, 1993). For instance, Buttner and Rosen (1988) found that loan officers associated the traits social conventions associate with successful entrepreneurs more closely with male business owners than with female business owners.[11] According to Stevenson (1986), women have been denied access to capital because they are associated to domestic roles that may be in contrast with the running of a company. Similarly, Fay and Williams (1993) argued that criteria used by lenders may discriminate against female business owners because women experience greater difficulties in acquiring the skills and knowledge necessary to conform to the criteria required by external lenders to grant a loan as women's work experience, education, socialization, etc., do not provide them opportunity to accumulate sufficient financial assets. Also women business owners may have less experience with financial management than men, as they have less opportunity to accumulate experience due to labour market segregation. Lack of experience may lead to differences in the financing patterns, as business owners with less experience may not know how they can acquire financial capital and whom they can contact for help and advice. Indeed, it has been suggested that women may not have any connection with an informal financial network that can provide support for financial issues (Olm *et al.*, 1988; Aldrich, 1989; Greene *et al.*, 2001). However, again this evidence cannot be considered final. Indeed, Buttner and Rosen (1989) found no evidence of sex stereotypes in the funding decisions of loan officers as male entrepreneurs were not favoured over female entrepreneurs. Also Buttner and Rosen (1992) found no significant gender difference in the perceptions of difficulty in obtaining a loan for a new venture. Haines *et al.* (1999) found that after controlling for firm size, age and sector, gender is not associated with the loan size, interest rate charged and collateral requirements. Uzzi (1999) found no significant differences in the cost of capital of loans to women- and men-owned businesses. Verheul and Thurik (2001), for example, focused on 2,000 entrepreneurial start-ups in 1994 in Holland (25 per cent of which were female) and concluded that females had less capital when starting the business but that there was no difference in the type of capital and that the proportion of equity and bank loans in women-led companies is the same as in those of their male counterparts (Verheul and Thurik, 2001). This may have an adverse effect on the perceived capacity of women to repay their loans, and so they may face greater difficulty in obtaining credit. Robb and Wolken (2002) found the business owner's characteristics and credit history as well as business risk, but not gender, prevented business owners from applying for a loan for fear of denial.

Also it has been suggested that women and men business owners differ with respect to their personal and business profile: they start and run businesses in different sectors, pursue different goals and structure their businesses in a different fashion (e.g. Fischer *et al.*, 1993; Chaganti and Parasuraman, 1996; Verheul and Thurik, 2001). Therefore it is possible that differences in business attributes may lead to differences in business financing. It appears that differences in the size of loans to women-owned businesses and men-owned businesses may be due to differences in business characteristics such as size, age, risk and industry rather than to gender (Riding and Swift, 1990; Orser *et al.*, 1994; Fabowale *et al.*, 1995; Haines *et al.*, 1999; Robb and Wolken, 2002; Storey, 2004). For instance women-owned companies are typically smaller than those owned by men (Riding and Swift, 1990; Orser *et al.*, 1994, 2000; Fabowale *et al.*, 1995; Coleman and Carsky, 1996; Coleman, 2000). Indeed, Robb and Wolken (2002) found women-owned businesses were significantly smaller than men-owned businesses in terms of employment, assets and sales. It is known that smaller businesses typically have greater difficulty in securing bank loans (Fabowale *et al.*, 1995; Storey, 2004) and tend to pay higher interest (Brau, 2002) than larger businesses independently of the owner's gender. Indeed, Fabowale *et al.* (1995) argued that although gender is not a determinant of the credit terms, it is highly correlated with the size of the business – women-owned businesses have less collateral, and an unproven track record relative to businesses owned by men. Also banks incur greater costs to evaluate and monitor small businesses as for small loans, the profit margin is not justified by the costs, and so banks may decline loans to small businesses or make the terms more stringent (Orser *et al.*, 1994; Haines *et al.*, 1999). The age of the company is another characteristic that may explain the differences in access to credit by women entrepreneurs. Women-owned businesses were found to be significantly younger than those owned by men (Riding and Swift, 1990; Coleman and Carsky, 1996; Haines *et al.*, 1999; Coleman, 2000; Robb and Wolken, 2002); Brau (2002) finds that older firms pay a significantly lower interest rate than younger firms. Of course, because of the age of the company, Robb and Wolken (2002) found that women-owned businesses had significantly shorter relationships with their lending institutions than did businesses owned by men (Bornheim and Herbeck, 1998). Because the length of the lending relationship affects the price and availability of credit (Uzzi, 1999; Berger and Udell, 2002a; Brau, 2002), a shorter lending relationship may influence the application for and the approval of loans, as well as the loan terms.

A third characteristic that may explain differences in bank lending to men- and women-owned businesses is the industry in which the company operates. Women-owned firms are more likely to operate in retail and services than firms owned by men (Belcourt *et al.*, 1991; Buttner and Rosen, 1992; Fabowale *et al.*, 1995; Coleman and Carsky, 1996; Coleman, 2000; Robb and Wolken, 2002), and this influences the type of credit the company needs. Indeed, service-based companies may require little financing as these companies will not be very capital intensive.[12] Also, women-owned businesses are typically considered riskier than those owned by men (Riding and Swift, 1990; Fabowale *et al.*, 1995; Coleman and Carsky, 1996; Robb and Wolken, 2002) because they tend to be smaller, younger and typically to have lower growth rates than companies owned by men (Riding and Swift, 1990; Fabowale *et al.*, 1995). Coleman (2000) noted that if women-owned businesses are perceived as riskier than businesses owned by men, they may be denied credit or offered credit on less favourable terms. The location of the business may also influence the availability of capital. Home-based businesses may be less successful in gathering external funds than businesses located outside the home, because they tend to be younger and less profitable (Edwards and Field-Hendrey, 1996). Also, financial institutions may see women owners of home-based businesses as an extension of their role as homemaker (Loscocco and Smith-Hunter, 2004), and therefore view them as less attractive customers.

What conclusions can be drawn from this short literature review? Most of the literature focuses on the financial constraints that women-owned firms face once these have been set up. However, from this literature the evidence in favour of financial discrimination is not strong. Indeed, it appears that once the firms' characteristics (size, age and sector) are controlled for, no evidence of financial discrimination against women-led firms can be found. This suggests that once the firms (owned by women) have been established and they are firmly in business, financial intermediaries allocate credit based on both/either the owner's track record and/or the availability of collateral and therefore independently of the owner's gender. Does this imply that finance constraints do not play any role in conditioning the formation of new firms owned by women? This would be a rather optimistic view. Indeed, I conjecture that more likely, financial constraints condition the individuals' probability of applying for external funding at the start-up stage. Indeed, it is important not to forget that potential borrowers can self-select themselves and decide not to apply for loans if they expect their application to be rejected by the external funders. This may reflect a correct assessment because the applicants do not possess the attributes (income, collateral) required by lenders. Alternatively these potential applicants may have incorrectly concluded that their applications would have been rejected when in fact they would have been approved. These considerations suggest that to clearly understand the impact of financial constraints on the creation of new firms by women, it is important to quantify the extent to which internal self-selection prevents potential female borrowers from applying for funds at the start-up stage, rather than focusing on firms that are already in business. However, the evidence so far on the impact of credit constraints on potential start-ups is relatively limited and somewhat conflicting and this is because it is quite difficult to evaluate the impact of financial constraints at the start-up stage where the firm does not exist.

2.4 Conclusions

This chapter has reviewed the rich literature on asymmetric information in the credit market and its impact on both the properties of the competitive equilibrium and the firms' productive activities. Of course this survey is not meant to be exhaustive and indeed I have only considered the literature that is mostly relevant for the following chapters. The starting point of this literature is the seminal paper by Stiglitz and Weiss (1981) which has characterized the main features of the competitive equilibrium in a credit market affected by both adverse selection and moral hazard and has improved our understanding of the functioning of credit markets under asymmetric information along with our understanding of how credit is allocated in this type of market. Imperfect information generates an equilibrium in the credit market where interest rates are inadequate to clear the market demand for loans. Therefore, to resolve asymmetric information problems, lenders utilize non-price mechanisms to ration loans based upon the characteriztics of the applicants or of the investment project itself. Therefore, the resulting equilibrium will be characterised by credit rationing where potential borrowers that are willing to accept the current credit conditions will not have access to external funding. Afterwards, economic research has evolved in two ways: on the one hand, theory has tried to identify the conditions under which the optimal properties of the competitive equilibrium can be restored in the credit market. On the other hand, the empirical literature has tried to test the implications of credit rationing on firms' productive activities and new business formation. Indeed, the presence of credit rationing increases the cost of external borrowing for firms and therefore firms may reduce their demand for investment if their financial reserves are not sufficient to fund their investment projects. Also, credit rationing may reduce the number of start-ups in the economy as potential entrepreneurs (not endowed with sufficiently large personal wealth) may not have access to external funding, again because of the prohibitively high cost of borrowing. Also, as personal characteristics condition the borrower's decision to grant a loan, then finance constraints will be more binding for women as they rarely have control over financial resources.

Generally speaking, the economic literature that looks at the relationship between economic outcomes and financial constraints is characterized by a recurring theme: financial constraints are "bad" as they alter the incentives structure economic agents are exposed to in such a way that the resulting market equilibrium is inefficient. Also they prevent potentially profitable and welfare-enhancing projects from being funded and allow borrowers' personal characteristics (that do not necessarily have any bearing on the future profitability of a project) to affect the market equilibrium. For instance, financial constraints increase the cost of borrowing and this way they depress firms' investment expenditure with the result that the economy-wide accumulated stock of capital may well be below the efficient level. Financial constraints have an adverse impact on new business formation in such a way that only individuals endowed with a certain level of personal wealth can opt for starting a new company. At a macroeconomic level, financial constraints can help to amplify negative productivity shocks as financially constrained firms will see their balance sheet position deteriorate very fast during a recession and this will increase even more the cost of external borrowing reinforcing the negative impact on the firm's level of production (Greenwald *et al.*, 1984; Gertler, 1988; Greenwald and Stiglitz, 1988; Greenwood and Williamson, 1989; Calomiris and Hubbard, 1990). At the same time, though, there exists a small empirical literature that identifies a positive impact of financial constraints on firms' productivity (Nickell and Nicolitsas, 1999). Equally, another contradiction emerges in the literature on financial constraints, gender and self-employment as mostly empirical studies in the field cannot find final evidence that supports the hypothesis that women are discriminated against in the credit market. Indeed, it is clear that the evidence in favour of financial discrimination is not strong and it appears that once the business characteristics are controlled, no evidence of financial discrimination against women can be found (see Carter *et al.*, 2001).

How to reconcile these two different sets of results? Is it possible to reach an overall conclusion on the direction of the impact that financial constraints can have on economic outcomes? I argue that these apparent contradictions between the positive and the negative impact of finance constraints on economic outcomes can be solved once financial constraints are considered as mechanisms that affect the ex-post distribution of the surplus generated in a relationship. This interpretation has the advantage that it allows clarification of the mechanisms through which finance constraints can have a positive impact on performance. Indeed, consider a financially constrained firm; the direct effect of these financial constraints is obviously that of increasing the cost of capital and therefore reducing the investment expenditure. However, the impact of financial constraints may be felt more by workers than by the owners of the firm as these reduce the wage bonus rather than the dividends to the shareholders. So, one additional consequence of the financial constraints could be that of reducing the workers' effort. In this case, the distribution of the rents is shifted in favour of the shareholders following an increase of the financial constraints and this will change the workers' behaviour ex-post. Also, if this interpretation of finance constraints is accepted, then it is possible to make predictions on the channels through which finance constraints can exert a positive impact on productivity. It is accepted that productivity itself is a complex concept, as it is made of two components, technical efficiency and technical change. On which component of total factor productivity do financial constraints act? Do they reduce the technical inefficiency or do they affect adversely the innovation activity and so technical change? Also, the positive impact of financial constraints may be limited though by the presence of increasing product market competition. What are the mechanisms behind these results? Also, why do financial pressure and increasing product market competition act as substitutes, rather than reinforcing each other?

Equally, I claim that financial constraints affect negatively the rate of formation of new firms led by women by conditioning the individuals' probability of applying for external funding at the start-up stage. This is possible because female applicants expect the terms of the loan agreement to be in favour of the financial institutions and therefore they are aware that most of the generated surplus will be appropriated (entirely or mostly) by the lender. So women prefer not to apply for external funding and therefore what it is observed in the aggregate is a small proportion of loans granted to female applicants. If this argument is accepted, then it is important to concentrate on the start-up stage (rather than on established firms) to clearly quantify the impact of financial constraints on women-led firms.

All these themes will be developed in the remaining chapters. Chapter 3 analyses the relationship between technical efficiency and financial pressure. I will first analytically show the conditions under which increasing financial pressure can improve a firm's technical efficiency. Then I will test the impact of finance constraints on technical efficiency using a panel of firms from Italian manufacturing over the period 1989–1994. In Chapter 4, I show that under specific circumstances, increasing financial pressure and increasing product market competition can have a complementary, positive impact on firms' technical efficiency unlike what the empirical literature in this area suggests. Indeed, I suggest this is the case in firms where for institutional reasons the individual remuneration is directly affected by the firm's performance and therefore there exists a clear channel through which the state of the competition in the product market and the credit conditions can directly affect the firm's performance. I argue this is the case of cooperatives where the surplus generated by the production is shared (totally or in part) among the workers. Afterwards, I test the extent to which financial pressure and increasing product market competition can either help or offset each other in improving cooperatives' technical efficiency, by using data on producers' cooperatives in the Italian wine industry. In Chapter 5, I analyse the impact that finance constraints have on women's start-ups. I suggest that women expect to face substantial financial constraints if trying to have access to external funding to set up their entrepreneurial activity. So a self-selection mechanism is at work where the probability an applicant has of approaching external funders is affected by its gender and its ethnic background. By using data on English start-ups drawn from the *Household Survey of Entrepreneurship*, 2003, I will first evaluate the extent to which finance constraints have an adverse impact on the probability of being self-employed and then whether these are compounded by gender and ethnic background. In a second model, I will try to quantify the extent to which our two main variables of interest (gender and ethnic background) have an impact only on the probability individuals have of experiencing financial constraints (and not on the career choice per se), so that only those who do not experience financial constraints can then become self-employed. Finally, I will test whether gender and ethnicity affect mainly the access to external finance, while the self-employment choice is influenced by other factors (like previous experience as self-employed, current employment status and so on) that are independent of both gender and ethnicity.

3 Technical efficiency and finance constraints

An empirical analysis for Italian manufacturing, 1989–1994

3.1 Introduction

In the previous chapter it has been established that the main impact of credit rationing (in equilibrium) on a firm is that of creating a wedge between the cost the firm has to bear to acquire external funds and the cost of the firm's internally generated funds. There are many reasons for this: lenders may incur additional costs in order to assess the creditworthiness of the potential borrowers; also they may need to evaluate the potential collateral that potential borrowers can offer to guarantee the loans and eventually monitor the loan's position once this has been granted. Obviously all the costs related to these activities are transferred onto the borrowers and this makes external funds more expensive than internally generated funds. One implication of this wedge between the costs of internal and external financial resources is that firms will give priority to internal funds to finance their productive activities, as obviously they tend to be cheaper than external funds. There is also another implication of credit rationing (that has not been thoroughly explored in the previous chapter): indeed it is also usually believed that it makes financially constrained firms more vulnerable to negative external shocks than firms that are not credit constrained (Fischer, 1934). The argument runs as follows: assume a negative external shock (like a fall in total factor productivity or an increase in the general level of interest rate) hits the economy. This has two implications on a firm: (a) it reduces the firm's current net worth together with the value of the financial resources generated internally; this has the immediate impact of reducing the resources that can be used either to fund investment or as collateral; (b) the debt to net worth ratio (a commonly used measure of bankruptcy probability) increases following the fall in the firm's net worth and this will increase the cost of borrowing (as banks will consider it riskier to fund the firm's investment projects than before), so reinforcing the negative impact of the original productivity shock on the availability of external resources.

On these occurrences, how do firms react? One possibility is to cut back temporarily on the level of production and investments so to reduce the operating costs. However, this option assumes that the firm is exposed only to one type of distortion (namely, the credit constraint) and that because of this the firm has to cut current expenditures. Indeed, in the real world, firms face multiple distortions and these may interact in such a way that it, in fact, becomes possible and profitable for a firm that is exposed to a tightening of its credit conditions to reduce slack in relation to some other distortion, and thereby as a net result improve its performance. For instance, firms that are financially constrained can also suffer from "organizational slack" or technical inefficiency for reasons that are related to the internal organization of the firm. So if the conditions at which a firm can have access to external credit are becoming less favourable, firms may prefer to reduce internal inefficiencies to generate additional financial resources that can be used to offset the tightening of the financial conditions. The next question then becomes: what are the sources of inefficiency within a firm? I assume these are related to the firm's internal organization. There are many reasons why a company may appear inefficient. Slack may be created by the lack of alignment of interests among different agents working in the firm. For instance, it is well known that managers may pursue objectives that are not the same as shareholders' and that because of the split between ownership and control (typical of the modern capitalist firm) managers may have some freedom to pursue their interests (Hermalin, 1992; Martin, 1993). In this process, they may decide to over-invest in some type of inputs (for instance capital) as in this case the appropriation of private benefits may be easier than otherwise; also in the presence of the effort–leisure trade-off, they may decide to enjoy more leisure than would be optimal for the firm. Inefficiency can also arise because of the bargaining process between workers and the owners of the firm (Haskel and Sanchis, 2000). The bargaining assumption is a natural one in labour markets where workers are unionized and wages are explicitly bargained over. In this type of model, workers attempt to appropriate some of the available surplus by bargaining with the firm higher wages and/or lower effort; the resulting equilibrium may entail more or less effort provided by the workers according to the union's bargaining power.

In both cases, a firm will appear inefficient because low effort causes the output to be below the maximum effort frontier. So, a negative shock to the firm with a consequent increase in the bankruptcy probability will mean for the worker an enhanced risk of losing the job and for the manager the loss of the financial benefits attached to his/her position with the firm. In both cases, both/either workers and/or managers may anticipate these negative outcomes and therefore may decide to increase their effort with the result that the firm's efficiency will increase. In real life, we can expect a mixture of the two effects to be at work and actually which of the two prevails depends ultimately on the bargaining power of both workers and managers. However, both cases, though, entail a clear empirical prediction: increasing financial pressure (due to a permanent negative shock) induces a firm to improve technical efficiency as long as there is some technical inefficiency in the organization.

These considerations set the agenda for this chapter. The purpose of this chapter is twofold: first, I want to formalize the relationship between finance constraints and technical efficiency in firms that have some organizational slack. Indeed, I consider a firm that uses both the manager's effort and capital as its inputs. Here I assume that inefficiency arises because of the mismatch of preferences between the manager's and the ownership of the firm. Indeed, managers can choose their level of effort so as to maximize their utility defined over the effort–leisure trade-off, while the ownership is obviously interested into maximizing the firm's profits. However, managers are paid only a fraction of their profits (performance-related payment) and this creates the conditions for a potential hold-up problem where managers will "hold-up" their effort as they anticipate they will not be able to appropriate all the benefits generated by their work. I show that the tightening of the credit constraints gives the manager the incentive to increase effort as (s)he anticipates that these can have an adverse effect on his share of profits. This way, inefficiency reduces as long as capital and effort substitute each other. Indeed, as the worsening of financial conditions reduces the availability of capital, the manager may decide to increase his effort as long as it can offset the negative impact of the finance constraints on the firm's production level. In the second part of the chapter, I consider the empirical evidence in support of the hypothesis that increasing financial constraints can reduce inefficiency. Therefore I test whether this is the case by using a sample of firms from Italian manufacturing over the period 1989–1994; then I will measure technical efficiency by estimating a best-practice frontier for each sector of the manufacturing, where the mean of the inefficiency distribution is conditioned on the measures of finance constraints.

The structure of the chapter is the following. In Section 3.2, I present the model showing the impact of credit constraints on technical efficiency. The empirical model is introduced in Section 3.3 while the data, the variables and the empirical results are presented and commented on in Section 3.4. Finally, some concluding remarks are offered in Section 3.5.

3.2 Technical efficiency and finance constraints: a partial equilibrium approach

Consider an industry with $I = 1, \ldots, N$ firms. I assume that all firms have limited access to the credit market (which means that they do not have sufficient financial capital to rent the desired amount of physical capital) and are internally inefficient. The firms in this industry are exposed to different credit constraints; also I assume that some firms are more efficiently organized than others. In the Introduction to the chapter I have outlined the many reasons why a firm is inefficient; however, here I assume that the inefficiency derives from the hold-up problem due to the fact that the manager of the firm has to make costly investments in the organization of the firm for which he can only hope to recoup a fraction of the return through its salary. However, some firms will be more efficient than others as they may be more successful at inducing the manager to align his interests to those of the firm. The model shows that a tightening of the credit constraint in a particular firm, which is not currently on the frontier, can help to catch up with firms on the frontier because the manager is induced to invest more effort in the firm; in other words, the tightening of credit conditions for a firm can be followed by an increase of technical efficiency for this same firm at a given point in time. Each period the firm produces with the following (convex) production technology:

$$y_{i,t} = F(e_{i,t-1}, k_{i,t}),$$

or

$$y_{i,t} = ae_{i,t-1} - 0.5e_{i,t-1}^2 + bk_{i,t} + \gamma k_{i,t} e_{i,t-1} \quad a>0 \text{ and } \gamma ><0.$$

Output is being produced by two inputs (managerial effort and capital) and is being sold at an exogenously fixed price, normalized to 1. γ (which can be either positive or negative) indicates whether marginal product of effort vested in organization is more or less productive in a firm with access to more capital or not. First, $k_{i,t}$ is the amount of physical capital equipment rented from a competitive market at the price of 1. The expenditure has to be paid up front and thus has to be financed through credit. As mentioned above, I assume that the firm is credit rationed and that the maximum amount of financial capital available for firm i in period t is $\bar{k}_{i,t}$ and that this constraint is always binding. The debt is paid back in full at the end of each period and, without loss of generality, I assume that the interest rate is nil. Second, the manager provides effort: he has to decide on his effort one period before production takes place. Once the decision has been made, it cannot be undone immediately. The manager makes the decision in anticipation of how much capital can be rented in the future which in turn is determined by the credit constraint. To capture differences in the internal organization of different firms in a simple way, I assume that the manager in firm i is rewarded for organizing the production process by a share s_i of the net profit $y_{i,t} - k_{i,t}$. This can be thought as representing an incomplete contracting situation where, after production has taken place, the manager and the owners of the firm negotiate about the share of the surplus that the manager should retain. In this situation a standard hold-up problem arises and so the parameter s can then be interpreted as a measure of the inefficiency in the internal organization of the firm.

The per period utility function of the manager is:

$$u_{i,t} = c_{i,t} - 0.5e_t^2$$

and his budget constraint is $c_{i,t} \square w_{i,t} \square s_i(y_{i,t} - k_{i,t})$ Life-time utility is then:

$$U_i = \sum_{t=0}^{T} \delta^t [s_i(y_{i,t} - k_{i,t}) - 0.5e_t^2],$$

where δ is the discount rate and $e_{-1} = 0$. The b in the production function must be sufficiently large to insure that the firm will actually borrow money up to the limit $b + \gamma e_{i,t} > 1 + r$.

The model can be solved by backwards induction. In period 2, production takes place:

$$y_{2,i} = ae_{1,i} + 0.5e_{i,t}^2 + bk_{2,i} + \gamma \bar{k}_{2,i} e_{1,i}$$

and the manager's income is:

$$s_i(y_{2,i} - \bar{k}_{2,i}).$$

In period 1, the manager faces the problem:

$$e_{1,i}^* = \arg\max \delta s_i(y_{2,i} - \bar{k}_{2,i}) - 0.5e_{i,1}^2.$$

The first-order condition is:

$$\delta s_i(a - e_{1,i} + \gamma \bar{k}_{1,i}) - e_{1,i} = 0$$

and his optimal effort choice is:

$$e_{1,i}^* = \frac{\delta s_i(a + \gamma \bar{k}_{i,2})}{1 + \delta s}.$$

The manager's payoff in period 2 is denoted by V_2^*. In period 0, the manager faces a similar problem:

$$e_{0,i}^* = \arg\max \delta s_i(y_{1,i} - \bar{k}_{1,i}) - 0.5e_{i,0}^2 + \delta^2 V_2^*$$

and he chooses similarly. In both cases, the optimal effort is:[1]

$$e_{t,i}^* = \frac{\delta s_i(a + \gamma \bar{k}_{i,t+1})}{1 + \delta s_i} \text{ for } t = 0,1.$$

It can be easily checked that optimal effort increases if the finance constraints gets more binding as long as $\gamma < 0$. Indeed, the manager makes his effort decision based on his expectations about the availability of credit in the future. If he anticipates that more credit is going to be available in the future and thus more rented capital equipment is going to be available he may decide to spend more effort in the firm. In particular, he spends less effort if the marginal productivity of his effort is lower in an environment with more capital equipment available ($\gamma < 0$).

Consider now technical efficiency. $\hat{y}_t$ is the output produced in period t by the firm with the best practice technique supported by a combination of efficient internal organization (high s_i and lax external credit constraints (high $\bar{k}$). I can measure technical efficiency in firm i in period t by comparing it to this benchmark:

$$TE_{i,t} = \frac{y^*_{i,t}}{\hat{y}_t},$$

where $y^*_{i,t} = ae^*_{i,t-1} - 0.5(e^*_{i,t-1})^2 + b\bar{k}_{i,t} + \gamma\bar{k}_{i,t}e^*_{i,t-1}$ for t = 1,2.

My main interest is to find out how technical efficiency periods 1 and 2 in firm i thus defined is affected by a lasting, but unexpected change in the credit constraint in period 1. The fact that it is unexpected implies that it could not be taken into account when effort was decided in period 0. The fact that it is lasting implies that the manager, once he has observed the change in period 1, would wish to adjust his effort choice made in that period recognizing that credit conditions in period 2 could also have changed. To simplify the analysis, I assume that $\bar{k}_{1,i} = \bar{k}_{2,i} = \bar{k}_i$ initially. It is also important to note that the change in credit conditions is local to firm i, that is, it does not apply to all the other firms in the industry. Therefore, I can take the benchmark as given.

A change in the credit constraint can affect the firm's output through three channels. First, the direct effect is obvious: if more credit becomes available in a given period, more capital can be rented and more can be produced. The second effect is an interaction effect and its direction depends on the sign of γ. If $\gamma < 0$, more credit would reduce output through this channel because it crowds out the productive value of effort; if $\gamma > 0$, more credit would enhance the productive value of the effort. The third effect works through a change in effort in anticipation of changing credit conditions in the future. Thus, this effect cannot affect technical efficiency in period 1, but will have an impact on efficiency in period 2. Again the effect depends critically on the sign of γ. For $\gamma < 0$, the manager would want to spend less effort on organizing production because the extra rented capital makes such effort less productive at the margin. As a consequence, output would fall in period 2. The opposite happens, of course, if $\gamma > 0$. The overall impact on output is then determined by the interaction between these effects.

With this in mind, consider first what happens to technical efficiency in period 1. Since the decision on effort has already been made in period 0 based on the expected credit conditions, I get:

$$\frac{\partial TE_{i,t}}{\partial \bar{k}_i} = \frac{1 + \gamma e^*_{i,0}}{\hat{y}_1} = \frac{1}{\hat{y}_1}(b + \gamma \frac{\delta s_i(a + \gamma\bar{k}_i)}{1 + \delta s_i}).$$

Next, consider period 2. After the change has been observed in period 1, the manager can adjust his effort choice to accommodate the new environment in period 2. The change in technical efficiency in period 2 is therefore given by:

$$\frac{\partial TE_{i,2}}{\partial \bar{k}_i} = \frac{1}{\hat{y}_1}[(a - e^*_{i,1} + \gamma\bar{k}_i)\frac{\partial e^*_{i,1}}{\partial \bar{k}_i} + b + \gamma e^*_{i,1}].$$

Using the FOC from the manager's effort decision problem I get:

$$\frac{\partial TE_{i,2}}{\partial \bar{k}_i} = \frac{1}{\hat{y}_1}[\gamma(a+\gamma\bar{k}_i)\frac{\delta s_i(2+\delta s_i)}{(1+\delta s_i)^2}+b]$$

by substitution of the optimal effort decision at time 1. It is clear that technical efficiency increases in both periods if $\gamma \geq 0$. However, this is not the case when $\gamma < 0$. Indeed in this case it is possible to identify four values of γ such that:

1   Technical efficiency in period 1 is decreasing in the credit constraint for $\gamma \in (\underline{\gamma}_1, \bar{\gamma}_1)$ and non-decreasing otherwise.
2   Technical efficiency in period 2 is decreasing in the credit constraint for $\gamma \in (\underline{\gamma}_2, \bar{\gamma}_2)$ and non-decreasing otherwise.

For small values of $\gamma \in]\bar{\gamma}_2, 0[$, technical efficiency increases in both periods because the interaction effect and the effort effect are small. For values of γ smaller than γ_1, the effort effect is sufficiently large to ensure that technical efficiency in period 2 falls, while technical efficiency in period 1 increases unless $\gamma < \bar{\gamma}_1$ because the interaction effect is not strong enough to dominate the direct effect. For γ yet lower, technical efficiency in both periods falls as the interaction effect is now sufficient to overcome the direct effect. Interesting, for very low values of γ, technical efficiency increases in both periods. The reason is that effort is very low and the interaction effect is dampened for that reason. Thus, there is a non-monotonic relationship between γ and the impact of credit constraints on technical efficiency. The most realistic case is the one with $\gamma > \bar{\gamma}_2$. This is the case where the interaction effect in itself is not sufficient to overcome the direct effect (and thus technical efficiency in period 1 is enhanced by the availability of more credit) while the combination of the effort effect and the interaction effect is sufficient to reduce technical efficiency in period 2. So in this case a restriction in the available credit reduces output immediately, but the manager in anticipation of the lack of machinery in the next period puts more effort into organizing production. This compensates for the lack of capital and may in some cases more than compensate. If so, technical efficiency improves in the next period.

3.3 The empirical analysis

In the previous section I have discussed the theoretical possibility that the tightening of financial constraints can have a positive impact on technical efficiency. This hypothesis will be tested on a sample of firms drawn from Italian manufacturing, from 1989 to 1994. A simple way to test this hypothesis is to derive a firm-level measure of technical efficiency and then relate the movements of this indicator to variations in the firms' availability of financial resources. A commonly used method to measure technical inefficiency is by estimating the gap between a firm's performance and the best practice performance in the industry.

In turn this can be measured by using the so-called stochastic frontier analysis where the measures of (in)efficiency are computed from the residual of the regression model (see Appendix D for a short survey on the frontier estimation techniques). The format of the empirical analysis is straightforward enough. I will estimate a best practice frontier for each sector where the firm's mean inefficiency is conditioned on the measures of financial constraints.

However, as the empirical analysis will be conducted on Italian data, it is worth providing some information about the structure of the Italian economy, along with some historical information that will serve an informative purpose for those readers not acquainted with recent Italian economic history. Also, the focus of this survey is on the evolution of the manufacturing system as this is the object of the empirical analysis carried out in the following sections.

3.3.1 Some features of Italian manufacturing

Historically the Italian manufacturing system is characterized by an even geographic distribution of firms between North and South and the prevalence of small and medium-sized firms (Graziani, 1992). These characteristics are confirmed when analysing the data collected by the Mediocredito Centrale. Table 3.1 presents the distribution of firms according to the number of employees in 1994 while Table 3.2 gives some information about the distribution of firms among the four Italian principal geographic areas, as defined by ISTAT (Italian Statistical Office).

In my data-set, most of the manufacturing firms are medium sized and they are concentrated mainly in two areas, the North West, whose industrial development goes back to the nineteenth century, and the North East whose manufacturing has expanded recently during the 1980s. Central Italy and Southern Italy have lagged behind with a low percentage of manufacturing firms locating in these areas. Last, Table 3.2 presents the distribution of firms across the so-called Pavitt sectors. These are the specialized supplier sector, the scale intensive sector, the supplier dominated sector and the high-tech sector.[2] The Pavitt classification divides firms according to their ability of receiving or transferring technology from and to other firms. Therefore, high-tech and scale-intensive sectors group firms usually transferring technology to other firms.

Table 3.1 Distribution of firms by employees, 1994

Employees	Percentage
11–20	20
21–50	24
51–250	40
251–500	7
>500	9

Source: Capitalia (former Mediocredito Centrale Database), 1997.

Table 3.2 Distribution of firms across Pavitt sectors, 1994

Sector	Percentage
Supplier-dominated sector	45
Scale-intensive sectors	35
Specialized supplier sectors	16
High-tech sectors	4

Source: Capitalia (former Mediocredito Centrale Database), 1997.

Firms belonging to the supplier-dominated sector usually depend on firms of the high-tech and scale-intensive sectors for their technological advances. The specialized supplier sector groups firms with exclusive relationships with the high-tech and scale-intensive sectors.

This table shows the prevalence of supplier-dominated activities in Italian manufacturing. Indeed, they are about 45 per cent of the whole of manufacturing, while the scale-intensive sector is 35 per cent of manufacturing. Specialized supplier sector and high-tech sector are very small with only 16 per cent and 4 per cent of firms.

3.3.2 An overview of the Italian economy, 1989–1994

To better understand the evolution of the Italian economy from 1989 to 1994, it is important to start describing the main features of the economy during the 1980s. Between 1983 and 1989, the growth in GDP in Italy was one of the highest in Europe, ranging from 3.5 to 4 per cent. Employment rose accordingly, without, however, bringing about any significant fall in unemployment. Indeed, the rate of unemployment went on growing after the rise of the early 1980s, only beginning to stabilize at the end of this period. Also, this period was characterized by a steady (positive) inflationary differential relative to most other European countries, which, given the adhesion to the EMS, led to a situation of latent external constraint and to the need of attracting foreign capital flows through high interest rates. High inflation and interest rates, grafted to the prolonged failure to reduce inefficiencies and excess public expenditure and to curb tax evasion, meant that the budget deficit remained high throughout these years, notwithstanding attempts at fiscal restraint towards the end of this period (Graziani, 1992; Banca d'Italia, 1997).

In 1989, while structural difficulties due to external and internal imbalances and inflation have maintained their strength, the rate of GDP growth began to take a slower pace. GDP growth in 1989 was close to 3.1 per cent. Despite fairly rapid growth in employment, the unemployment rate remained flat at around 12 per cent. Domestic demand growth was still rapid, driven by both consumption and investment demand. Indeed, the rate of growth of consumption was buoyant and the investment expansion continued in 1989 when it grew from 5 per cent to 6 per cent. The trend of expenditure in fixed investment differed according to the type of investment. Investment in plant and equipment was boosted by rationalization measures and there was an increase in capacity-expanding investment. This pick-up in investment in plant and equipment was stimulated by the brighter overall outlook for demand and by the steady rise in capacity utilization rates in industry. The expansion of rationalization investment, the fact that an increasing amount of work was contracted out and the easing of the terms of employment, particularly in small enterprises, allowed the private sector to respond flexibly to increasing demand.

The return to a distribution of national income more favourable to business had a positive impact on investment. The increased share of profits in national income was reflected in the self-financing/investment ratio. However, this overall trend masked different situations according to the size of the enterprise. In the manufacturing sector, small and medium-sized enterprises financed their investment to a large degree by means of bank loans, which meant that their investment was sensitive to changes in interest rates. The major enterprises improved their financial position during the 1980s which made them independent of external sources of finance. Therefore the interest burden was reduced successfully by these firms. This situation was reflected in the amount of investment made by the two groups of firms: the investment by small/medium sized enterprises grew by 2 per cent whereas for larger firms it grew by nearly 16 per cent. Manufacturing added value growth rate was up to 5.4 per cent. This was due to both the capital goods production (stimulated by the growth of investment in plant and equipment) and the production of consumer durables.

However, the current account deficit increased sharply to 1.4 per cent of GDP for the year as a whole. As in other OECD countries, inflation accelerated between the third quarter of 1988 and mid-1989. These two factors, together with the prospect of a surge in the government deficit, prompted the authorities to raise interest rates and to take immediate fiscal consolidation measures. The interest rate differentials between Italy and its partners led to capital inflows which pushed up the value of the lira until late summer, thus eroding competitiveness. As Italy did not participate to the general upward movement in European interest rates in October 1989, the Italian lira fell rapidly against the German currency. Afterwards the Italian economy was caught in a period of slow growth, well below its potential. Under the combined impact of high interest rates in defence to the external value of the Italian lira and an effective real appreciation of the currency, the level of demand directed towards the home market fell increasingly short of growing output capacity, leading to increasing unemployment from already high structural levels. The slowdown of growth was worsened by the failure of the government to reverse the rapidly deteriorating trend in public finance.

However, until mid-1992, the weakening of economic growth was counterbalanced by real private consumption which, supported by large real wage gains and a drop in the savings ratio, expanded fast. With net exports shrinking, squeezed profit margins and real interest rates high, entrepreneurs curtailed capital spending. The weakness of output growth has not evenly spread across sectors. In industry, added value fell by 0.6 per cent in 1991 with larger declines occurring in both medium-sized and large enterprises, located in the North. In the first half of 1992, with exports growing, industry was pulling haltingly out of its slump. By the first quarter of 1992, industrial employment declined by 2.6 per cent from its peak level in the second quarter of 1991. The rise in the labour market slack was initially not reflected in higher unemployment as discouraged unemployed left the labour force. The fall in output, begun in autumn 1992, seemed to have bottomed out in the summer as a result of the rebound of exports. Internally, a collapse of consumer and business confidence depressed the level of domestic demand: private consumption declined in the face of real wage losses, while gloomier output prospects accelerated the decline in gross fixed investment. In the closing months of 1992, the Italian economy dipped into recession with GDP falling by an annualized 1.2 per cent in the second half of 1992. Pulled down by falling gross fixed investment and lower net exports, the rise in real GDP slipped below 1 per cent for 1992, half a percentage point below the EU average. Falling rates of return on capital, high real interest rates and a worsening business climate depressed fixed investment. Private consumption levelled off in the second half of the year under the combined impact of falling real wages, a growing labour market and a deteriorating consumer confidence. As a result, domestic demand began to decline, pushing up employment from already high structural levels. Misgivings about the conduct of fiscal policy had built a strong downward pressure on the lira. Despite sharp increases in key lending rates in response to this, official reserves went on being depleted, setting the stage for the exit of Italy from the EMS and a sharp depreciation of the lira (around 20 per cent in the last months of 1992).

The growth performance in 1992 would have been even weaker had it not been for the unusual speed with which imports responded to the lira depreciation. The economic downturn gathered pace in the autumn of 1992 as private consumption expenditure began to decline, compounding the drop in fixed investment. Several factors contributed to the fall in private consumption: increased taxation, pessimism about income growth and employment prospects. By the end of 1992, industry had moved into deep recession: industrial added value fell by 2.1 per cent in the second half of 1992 and industrial investments for the year as a whole declined by more than 9 per cent. With stocks of finished goods reduced to more normal levels, and foreign demand picking up in response to the currency depreciation, the production had slowed down since the beginning of 1993, leaving industrial output in the first seven months of the year 4.7 per cent lower than a year earlier. Capacity was 2 per cent points lower. In an attempt to restore profitability, large industrial firms reduced employment by nearly 6 per cent to mid-1993.

In 1993 output dropped by 0.7 per cent, a steep fall in total domestic demand, largely offset by net export buoyancy. All sectors suffered from output declines, production shrinking by 2.4 per cent in industry. Within the industrial sector, small and medium-sized firms with less than 200 employees cut back output by a disproportionate amount, reflecting an adverse trend in the chemical and metal industries. Gross fixed investment plunged by 11 per cent, pulled down by declining profitability, worsening output prospects and a freeze on public investments. Investment in machinery and equipment were hard hit by the recession. Output losses were cut by the surge in net exports. Real export growth doubled, stimulated by strong gains in competitiveness and depressed domestic demand. A falling interest rate, good inflation performance and signs of stronger market growth abroad were crucial elements in turning economic activity around, raising business confidence in the closing months of 1993. By the autumn of 1994, most conjunctural indicators pointed to a vigorous economic expansion being well established.

With the recovery of investment in machinery and equipment, activity rise became more broadly based, having been initially focused on exports. Real GDP expanded by 2.2 per cent in 1994, the best performance since 1989, as domestic demand rebounded, despite some slowing signs of activity, in the first half, mainly as a consequence of stock adjustment and hesitant consumption. Output gains were slow to translate into employment increases. While the recession was shorter and steeper than its antecedents, the rebound in economic activity was slow to build up momentum. Exports have been strongly boosted by buoyant export markets and gains in competitiveness. Compared with earlier cyclical episodes, business fixed investment responded to the export surge with an unusually long lag. Uncertainty about the extent and durability of the upswing resulted in relatively long lags between output and employment developments, impacting negatively on consumption. The recovery was concentrated in the industry and market services where output gains outweighed continued declines in the construction sector.

To summarize, the Italian economy has been subject to a considerable evolution in the period under examination. Indeed, in 1989 the rate of growth of GDP began to take a slower pace even though domestic demand growth was still rapid. The distribution of national income more favourable to business had a positive impact on investment and many rationalization measures were made with a fast increase in capacity-expanding investment. However, the increase in the current account deficit, together with an increase in inflation and misgivings in the Government fiscal policy, led to a further weakening of the economic growth culminating in the recession of 1992 and 1993. Industrial added value fell very fast together with the industrial investment. In an attempt to restore profitability, large industrial firms reduced employment considerably. The relaunch of the economy was possible only in 1994 thanks to the real export growth stimulated by strong gains in competitiveness. Therefore, by the end of 1994, most business cycle indicators pointed to a vigorous economic expansion being well established.

3.3.3 The production frontier specification and the data

The model I use for estimation purposes is rather straightforward. I will estimate a parametric stochastic production frontier through the approach suggested by

Battese and Coelli (1995). This method estimates a stochastic production frontier where the mean of the inefficiency distribution is an explicit function of firm-specific factors that are assumed to influence the inefficiency levels. The advantage of this approach is that it allows us to compute the efficiency scores while controlling for the factors which influence the distribution of scores across the different observations.[3] I assume a translog functional form for the production function:

$$\ln y_{it} = \alpha_0 + \alpha_k \ln k_{it} + \alpha_{kk} \ln k_{it}^2 + 0.5\alpha_{kl} \ln k_{it} \ln l_{it} + \alpha_l \ln l_{it}$$
$$+ \alpha_{ll} \ln l_{it}^2 + \gamma t + 0.5\gamma t^2 + \mu_k \ln k_{it} t + \mu_l \ln l_{it} + \varepsilon_{it}$$

$$i = 1, \ldots, I \text{ and } t = 1, \ldots, T,$$

where k and l are the capital and labour respectively, t is the time trend, i denotes the number of firms and t the number of time periods. The time trend variable appears both as a second-order polynomial and associated with inputs. These terms and the corresponding parameters introduce second-order flexibility in the translog function and are used to identify technical change that is both neutral and embodied into the inputs.

The production frontier specification includes a composed error term:

$$\varepsilon_{it} = u^{it} - v^{it},$$

allowing for both firm-specific inefficiency effects, u^{it} and a stochastic noise v_{it} distributed as a $N(0, \sigma_v^2)$. The u^{it} reflects the shortfall of the firms relative to their own best practice in each period, where the best practice for the firm is determined by the frontier. The technical efficiency term is comprised of non-negative random variables that are assumed to be independently distributed as truncations of the $N(\delta z_{it}, \sigma_u^2)$ distribution, where z_{it} are the factors[4] that may influence the mean inefficiency in our sample of firms and δ is a vector of parameters to be estimated. I assume that the inefficiency effects are a linear function of the size of the finance constraints the firm is facing, so that the mean of the inefficiency distribution is directly affected by the firm's availability of financial resources. The production frontier is estimated using Maximum Likelihood, as in Battese and Coelli (1995). The firm-level technical efficiency score is then computed as:

$$TE^{it} = \exp(-\hat{u}_{it}).$$

In other words, I use a one-stage approach to the estimation of the firm's technical inefficiency as opposite to the two-stage approach that produces inconsistent estimates of the parameters of interest as the observations are not independent of each other. The empirical analysis has been conducted on a panel of 1,124 firms drawn from the Capitalia database, observed over the period 1989–1994. These firms have then been divided into the eight main

Table 3.3 Number of observations by sector

Sector	Number of observations
Extraction of metals	324
Transformation of metals	1,662
Food	258
Tobacco	486
Textiles	270
Leather	1,410
Wood	1,368
Paper	720

Source: Author's calculations.

sectors of Italian manufacturing namely the Extraction of Metals, Transformation of Metals, Food, Tobacco, Textiles, Leather, Wood and Paper.

Next, I have derived the measures of inputs and outputs of these firms. Following previous studies on the efficiency and productivity of the manufacturing sector (Siegel, 1995; Beenstock, 1997), I have measured output by the monetary added value. However, this figure has been deflated properly; the employed deflators have been derived by dividing the added value at constant prices by the added value at constant prices (namely, at 1990 prices). These two figures have been drawn from the Italian National Accounts, prepared by Golinelli and Monterastrelli (1990). The capital has been measured by the gross fixed capital stock. As this measure is available at market prices, it has been deflated by the deflator of the gross fixed investment for each sector provided by ISTAT (Italian Central Institute for Statistics). This last variable has been computed by dividing the gross fixed investment at current prices with the gross fixed investment at constant prices. The labour input has been finally measured by the average number of employees per firm.

Table 3.4 presents the average value of the deflated monetary added value, deflated gross fixed capital and number of employees divided by sectors and years.

A brief look at the data contained in this table shows that all the sectors have shared the same cyclical evolution in the period under consideration. In all sectors the growth of added value stopped in 1992 with the only exceptions being the sectors of Extraction and Transformation of Metals and Food. The employment shared the same cyclical pattern as the added value. In coincidence with the recession of 1992 and 1993, all sectors started a remarkable disinvesting process, pushed by the need of downsizing the productive structures. The effects of this process were, indeed, evident in the years immediately after the recession when the fixed assets increased in most sectors. However, from this evolution, the sectors of Extraction and Transformation of Metals were excluded: indeed, the productive capacity was remarkably reduced due to the need of downsizing the two sectors.

The next step is choosing the measures of finance constraints. The empirical literature on the relationship between finance constraints and firms'

Table 3.4 Average added value, average gross fixed capital and average number of employees by year and sector

Sector	Year	Added value	Fixed assets	Employees	Sector	Year	Added value	Fixed assets	Employees
Extraction of metals	1989	8,733	16,413	113	Textiles	1989	22,716	33,552	237
	1990	7,725	15,224	106		1990	11,860	18,232	160
	1991	9,368	21,287	115		1991	20,055	35,441	226
	1992	10,527	27,568	130		1992	12,550	19,287	152
	1993	10,192	23,925	119		1993	20,628	35,978	212
	1994	10,016	17,488	106		1994	18,223	30,518	185
Transformation of metals	1989	12,618	15,853	176	Leather	1989	42,476	73,507	696
	1990	7,973	12,063	129		1990	12,384	37,471	211
	1991	13,109	18,798	182		1991	3,972	8,719	120
	1992	12,614	15,032	278		1992	10,171	18,364	193
	1993	9,307	12,835	147		1993	8,886	17,839	186
	1994	12,750	15,117	183		1994	14,014	37,739	232
Food	1989	9,464	11,377	151	Wood	1989	8,013	6,055	202
	1990	10,430	14,287	162		1990	7,127	5,914	149
	1991	9,563	14,445	135		1991	8,057	8,004	162
	1992	13,276	13,298	176		1992	7,535	7,181	156
	1993	19,512	21,967	270		1993	6,644	6,107	134
	1994	19,910	16,682	273		1994	6,450	5,349	120
Tobacco	1989	16,269	30,895	207	Paper	1989	5,735	7,877	111
	1990	10,219	17,817	138		1990	5,669	8,337	105
	1991	21,219	40,664	186		1991	6,858	11,591	113
	1992	14,275	27,802	152		1992	7,184	12,946	113
	1993	14,400	30,688	156		1993	6,550	9,745	104
	1994	18,441	43,612	189		1994	6,772	9,574	112

Source: Author's calculations.

demand for investment offers useful suggestions. Two types of measures have been considered in this literature. The first proxies the size of the firms' financial constraints with the agency costs the firms face. Bernanke and Gertler (1989, 1990) suggested that the spread between a risky interest rate and a riskless interest rate on securities of the same maturity might indeed capture the agency costs of financial intermediation. Therefore they used the interest rate spread to parameterize the shadow cost of finance constraints in the Euler equation for the asymmetric information model and found a statistically significant relationship between the risky spread and the aggregate investment in the USA. However, this measure can be thought of as capturing the effect of aggregate shocks to internal net worth which might affect the shadow cost of finance and may not be suitable when trying to measure the firm-specific financial constraints. The second type of measures uses firm-specific measures of agency costs, such as the debt-to-equity ratio (DAR) and/or interest coverage ratios (ICR) (Whited, 1992; Ng and Schaller, 1996). In this case it is usual to distinguish between short- and long-run measures of finance constraints, where the former refers to constraints the firm may have in its operational expenses and the latter to constraints in its investment expenditures (and so the long-run expansion of the firm). The former variable is defined as the ratio between the market value of the firm's long-run debt and the market value of its total assets where the higher the ratio, the less external resources are available to the firm as its default risk is too high; so the firm is financially constrained. It can be considered as a measure of the firm's current demand for borrowing relative to its debt capacity, usually proxied by the market value of the firm. Given the reliance of finance-constrained firms on long-run debt to finance its investment expenditure, obviously the DAR is a measure of how much a firm is constrained in its expansion. For these reasons increases in the DAR (or a tightening of the available financial resources) are expected to have a positive impact on technical efficiency: if a firm is constrained in its access to external resources, then the only way to fund a potential expansion is by reducing internal inefficiencies. The picture is different for the ICR: this is the ratio of the firm's interest expenditures to the sum of interest expense plus cash-flow. The ratio will be higher for a firm that has encountered negative shocks that either reduce cash-flow or increase interest payments. In this respect, this ratio measures the extent to which a firm can rely on internal financial resources to fund its activities: a high ratio implies that the firm cannot generate sufficient funds and therefore in this case, the firm will be constrained in its operational expenses. The impact of this variable on efficiency is more ambiguous. An important aspect to consider in this respect is whether the negative shocks are permanent or temporary: if the negative shock is permanent, then an obvious way to increase internal resources is by reducing inefficiency. However, if the shock is temporary, the firm may not want to start an internal re-organization as the decrease of financial resources is deemed to be temporary. Table 3.5 shows the evolution over time of both DAR and ICR by sector.

Table 3.5 Average debt to asset ratio (DAR) and interest coverage ratio (ICR), by year and sector

Sector	1989	1990	1991	1992	1993	1994
DAR						
Extraction of metals	0.244567	0.231102	0.162587	0.148825	0.197445	0.177236
Transformation of metals	0.13456	0.144576	0.166047	0.185386	0.181739	0.215029
Food	0.18768	0.195161	0.211648	0.201381	0.204036	0.180864
Tobacco	0.13567	0.154365	0.15893	0.190042	0.168051	0.104423
Textiles	0.13896	0.138784	0.141875	0.129372	0.151704	0.11645
Leather	0.13569	0.134416	0.147011	0.129951	0.157379	0.11618
Wood	0.15679	0.169333	0.221098	0.22105	0.235448	0.22014
Paper	0.23564	0.239648	0.22791	0.193107	0.195135	0.152643
ICR						
Extraction of metals	0.54674	0.54678	0.55678	0.56879	0.56479	0.57879
Transformation of metals	0.59789	0.595114	0.561802	0.592066	0.641751	0.645156
Food	0.58968	0.595161	0.611648	0.601381	0.604036	0.580864
Tobacco	0.55678	0.554365	0.55893	0.590042	0.568051	0.504423
Textiles	0.57869	0.588145	0.602362	0.635997	0.663198	0.642574
Leather	0.5297	0.536329	0.543767	0.576809	0.593712	0.571138
Wood	0.61235	0.614947	0.598818	0.644008	0.666651	0.63928
Paper	0.46879	0.48153	0.527404	0.524301	0.591439	0.589461

Source: Author's calculations.

From the data contained in the table, it clearly emerges that the sectors are rather similar in terms of DAR: this means that firms generally decide to finance only a fixed share of their physical investment by debt as this proportion is regarded safe for the financial health of the firm. For the sector of Extraction of Metals, the DAR has decreased along time, with the only exception being 1993. The opposite trend can be found for the sector of Transformation of Metals, whose DAR has increased over time. In the Food industry, it continuously increased until 1991, while decreasing afterwards. In the Tobacco industry, the DAR increased until 1992, while decreased afterwards. More complicated is the behaviour of the DAR for the Textiles sector: indeed, it increased until 1991 and then decreased in 1992; however, it started increasing again in 1993 to fall down again in 1994. The Leather sector shared the same pattern. For the Wood sector, the DAR increased over time, while for firms in the Paper sector, DAR decreased continuously over time. As for the ICR there is no clear difference among sectors. In general all had a ratio of around 0.50 which implies that the interest expenses were very high given the firms' cash-flow. For the sector of Extraction of Metals, the ICR was generally constant across years. For the Transformation of Metals, the ICR was (more or less) the same until 1992 but increased in 1993 and 1994. For the Food Processing sector, the ICR grew from 1989 to 1991, while decreasing slightly afterwards. In the Tobacco industry, the ICR was more or less constant until 1992; however, in 1993 it started decreasing fast. For Textiles, it increased steadily until 1993 to decrease suddenly in 1994. The same pattern was shared by the Leather sector, where it increased until 1993 and then decreased in 1994. It increased until 1993 to decrease in 1994 in the Leather sector. In the Wood sector, the ICR had a more volatile pattern: it was constant until 1991 and then it increased again in 1992 and 1993. However, in 1994, it went down again. Finally in the Paper sector, the ICR increased constantly from 1989 till 1993, while it decreased slightly in 1994.

3.4 The econometric results

Table 3.6 presents the Maximum Likelihood Estimates of the production frontier for the eight industries.[5] For each industry, I have estimated two separate production functions where either DAR or ICR has been introduced among the *z*-variables. The reason for choosing this estimation strategy can be described as follows: the two variables DAR and ICR can have a different impact on technical efficiency. As specified above, DAR is a measure of how much a firm is constrained in its expansion and therefore it is expected to have a positive impact on technical efficiency: if a firm is constrained in its access to external resources, then the only way to expand is by reducing internal inefficiencies. The picture is different for the ICR. The impact of this variable on efficiency is more ambiguous. An important aspect to consider in this respect is whether the negative shock is considered to be permanent or temporary: if the negative shock is permanent, then an obvious way to increase internal resources is to reduce inefficiency. However, if the shock is deemed to be temporary, the firm may not want to start an internal re-organization in face of a temporary decrease of financial resources and may rather shed workers and investments temporarily. Therefore, given the potential different impact of DAR and ICR on technical efficiency, it is possible that technical efficiency change may go in different directions according to whether either DAR or ICR is included in the model.

Before estimating the production function, I have mean-corrected the data so that the first-order coefficients listed in Table 3.5 can be interpreted as elasticities, evaluated at the sample means. The main results can be summarized as follows. The value of the γ parameters (i.e. the ratio of σ_u^2 to the sum of σ_u^2 and σ_v^2) is significantly greater than zero across all sectors, indicating that the use of frontier estimators (rather than OLS estimators) is justified. First-order coefficients have the expected signs on behalf of the economic behaviour. The coefficients of the time trend variables (both as the second-order polynomial and associated with inputs) show that the sectors have experienced some sort of technical regress throughout the considered sample period, with the sectors of Extraction of Metals, Transformation of Metals, Textiles and Leather having a negative coefficient of the linear time trend and the sectors of Tobacco and Paper having a negative coefficient of the squared time trend. To test the significance of the coefficients of the technical change variables, I have conducted a likelihood ratio test which involves the calculation of:

$$LR = -2\left[LLF(H_0) - LLF(H_A)\right]$$

Table 3.6 Maximum likelihood estimates by sector

Variables	Parameters	t-ratio	Parameters	t-ratio
Extraction of metals				
Constant	8.74	88.04	8.69	121.38
K	0.25	4.86	0.26	4.76
L	0.57	6.89	0.56	6.66
K^2	0.093	8.04	0.092	6.86
L^2	0.014	3.95	0.012	3.06
T	−0.12	−1.93	−0.11	−2.28
t^2	0.02	2.15	0.02	2.52
tK	−0.01	−0.66	−0.01	−0.74
tL	0.04	1.81	0.04	1.95
KL	0.04	2.5	0.04	2.58
Constant	−4.88	−1.09	−7.06	−1.69
ICR	−2.2	−1.66	−	−
DAR	−	−	4.02	1.8
σ^2	1.18	1.38	0.86	2.22
γ	0.9	11.69	0.85	11.95
λ_1	29.6	−	26.6	−
λ_2	9.88	−	10.56	−
Mean efficiency	0.84	−	0.87	−
Average technical change	−0.056		−0.056	−
Transformation of metals				
Constant	3.7	239.69	3.7	237.41
K	0.11	10.72	0.11	11.3
L	0.36	37.14	0.34	25.29
K^2	0.007	0.007	0.005	0.004
L^2	0.004	0.004	0.004	0.003
t	−0.01	−0.03	−0.01	−0.34
t^2	0.01	1.07	0.01	1.39
tK	−0.01	−3.01	−0.01	−3.47
tL	0.01	2.28	0.01	2.79
KL	0.01	0.25	0.01	0.16
Constant	−7.23	−6.16	−6.21	−6.57
ICR	−1.68	−6.39	−	−
DAR	−	−	−1.01	−6.61
σ^2	0.8	6.61	0.79	7.08
γ	0.99	387.64	0.99	354
λ_1	19.72	−	17.84	−
λ_2	33.52	−	35.68	−
Mean efficiency	0.9	−	0.9	−
Average technical change	0.118	−	0.118	−
Food				
Constant	8.91	151.19	8.92	142.75
K	0.3	4.9	0.3	4.59
L	0.69	8.39	0.7	7.68
K^2	0.03	1.27	0.029	1.28
L^2	0.09	2.22	0.01	2.35

continued

Table 3.6 continued

Variables	Parameters	t-ratio	Parameters	t-ratio
t	0.03	0.98	0.03	0.93
t^2	0.01	0.4	0.01	0.36
tK	−0.03	−1.89	−0.03	−1.7
tL	0.04	2	0.04	1.64
KL	0.05	3.11	0.05	3.21
Constant	−14.86	−1.23	−16.26	−1.67
ICR	−4.86	−1.27	−	−
DAR	−	−	−0.02	−0.08
σ^2	3.33	1.25	3.98	1.72
γ	0.99	86.86	0.99	151.54
λ_1	38.08	−	30.58	−
λ_2	20.94	−	19.426	−
Mean efficiency	0.81	−	0.81	−
Average technical change	0.344	−	0.344	−
Tobacco				
Constant	8.54	109.04	8.52	113.22
K	0.4	7.11	0.4	7.01
L	0.64	9.27	0.64	9.06
K^2	0.04	2.66	0.043	2.68
L^2	0.039	1.13	0.04	1.15
t	0.09	1.81	0.09	1.94
t^2	−0.01	−0.83	−0.01	−0.89
tK	−0.03	−1.95	−0.03	−1.88
tL	0.02	0.91	0.02	0.83
KL	0.01	0.3	0.01	0.15
Constant	−10.23	−2.41	−3.46	−2.76
ICR	−3.22	−2.17	−	−
DAR	−	−	−4.03	−2.53
σ^2	1.69	2.84	0.98	3.67
γ	0.92	27.51	0.85	18.21
λ_1	2.3	−	3.1	−
λ_2	26.24	−	26.04	−
Mean efficiency	0.86	−	0.88	−
Average technical change	−0.903	−	−0.903	−
Textiles				
Constant	8.97	75.95	8.96	78.92
K	0.34	3.93	0.34	4.04
L	0.72	7.67	0.72	7.95
K^2	0.061	2.37	0.062	2.38
L^2	0.11	3.62	0.13	3.65
t	−0.03	−0.38	−0.02	−0.25
t^2	0.01	1.02	0.01	0.92
tK	−0.04	−2.04	−0.04	−1.99
tL	0.02	0.97	0.02	0.95
KL	0.01	0.76	0.01	0.74
Constant	−21.48	−1.08	−11.42	−0.62

continued

Table 3.6 continued

Variables	Parameters	t-ratio	Parameters	t-ratio
ICR	−4.86	−0.93	−	−
DAR	−	−	−7.54	−0.59
σ^2	6.93	1.13	5.42	0.63
γ	0.98	67.27	0.98	32.41
λ_1	16.86	−	19.54	−
λ_2	15.82	−	26.06	−
Mean efficiency	0.76	−	0.76	−
Average technical change	−0.545	−	−0.545	−
Leather				
Constant	8.72	220.25	8.73	193.04
K	0.34	12.78	0.35	13.99
L	0.61	17.81	0.62	17.96
K^2	0.039	4.86	0.036	4.67
L^2	0.073	4.55	0.069	4.37
t	−0.07	−2.55	−0.07	−2.53
t^2	0.01	3.29	0.01	3.29
tK	−0.03	−4.27	−0.03	−4.54
tL	0.03	2.94	0.03	2.89
KL	0.01	1.09	0.01	1.03
Constant	−13.89	−20.56	−12.8	−4.27
ICR	−0.01	−1.02	−	−
DAR	−	−	−0.77	−2.53
σ^2	3.03	21.86	2.9	4.48
γ	0.97	453.32	0.96	96.19
λ_1	65.9	−	68.94	−
λ_2	39.1	−	40.88	−
Mean efficiency	0.83	−	0.83	−
Average technical change	0.746	−	0.746	−
Wood				
Constant	8.14	157.68	8.15	154.42
K	0.35	11.7	0.35	11.85
L	0.66	16.54	0.66	16.77
K^2	0.008	1.11	0.007	1.13
L^2	0.019	1.14	0.018	1.24
T	0.02	0.59	0.02	0.48
t^2	0.01	0.37	0.01	0.49
tK	−0.02	−2.53	−0.02	−2.59
tL	0.01	0.67	0.01	0.73
KL	0.01	0.08	0.01	0.07
Constant	−17.75	−2.95	−15.76	−3.85
ICR	−0.33	−2.73	−	−
DAR	−	−	−1.58	−3.91
σ^2	4.88	3.13	4.61	4.16
γ	0.97	99.62	0.97	134.8
λ_1	92.5	−	92.8	−
λ_2	30.38	−	30.28	−

continued

Table 3.6 continued

Variables	Parameters	t-ratio	Parameters	t-ratio
Mean efficiency	0.79	–	0.79	–
Average technical efficiency	0.017	–	0.017	–
Paper				
Constant	8.13	149.89	8.14	141.32
K	0.23	6.95	0.23	7.05
L	0.82	16.62	0.82	16.73
K^2	0.05	6.39	0.049	6.35
L^2	0.07	3.83	0.05	3.56
T	0.05	1.3	0.04	1.22
t^2	−0.01	−0.55	−0.01	−0.42
tK	−0.02	−2.9	−0.02	−2.96
tL	0.03	2.77	0.03	2.75
KL	0.01	0.13	0.01	0.29
Constant	−14.47	−3.19	−12.91	−3.89
ICR	−0.27	−3.4	–	–
DAR	–	–	2.51	4.06
σ^2	3.17	3.37	2.54	4.21
γ	0.98	117.08	0.97	112.49
λ_1	75.4	–	75.12	–
λ_2	47.64	–	26.92	–
Mean efficiency	0.83	–	0.83	–
Average technical efficiency	−0.258	–	−0.258	–

where $LLF(H_0)$, $LLF(H_A)$ are the values of the log-likelihood function under the null and the alternative hypotheses, respectively. This statistic has an asymptotic Chi-square distribution, with degrees of freedom equal to the number of restrictions. The results of the tests are shown in Table 3.5. Generally speaking, technical change variables are significant for all sectors. Interestingly, the coefficients of the embodied technical change show that for all the sectors under consideration the technical change related to the stock of capital has been negative (Scott, 1991). These results point to the fact that for some sectors there has been some sort of technical regress. This is confirmed by looking at the average technical change experienced by the sectors over the sample period which is reported at the bottom of each table.[6] Interestingly, most sectors report a negative technical change. This result can be understood by recalling that in the sample period Italian manufacturing was affected by a sharp recession that hit the economy in the period 1992–1993. It is well known that during recessions the productive structure of an economy goes through a process of change where old techniques are eliminated and substituted by new techniques, mostly embodied in the stock of capital in both cases (Caballero and Hammour, 1994, 1996). In this case, during recessions, both the rates at which new techniques are either created or destroyed change and what it is observed in the aggregate is the net result of these two contrasting forces. Obviously it may happen that the process of destruction is faster than the one of creation and this implies that the sector is experiencing "negative" technical change (or technical regress). This is exactly what has happened in the sectors experiencing technical regress: during the recession the destruction of old techniques has been the prevalent force over creation. In a sense, these results hint that tighter finance constraints do not have any bearings on technical change, which is an important dimension of a company's performance. Indeed, during a recession when the availability of financial resources is scarce, a firm prefers to reduce technical inefficiency rather than to engage in changes of the technology to compensate the reduction in financial resources. Interestingly, the size of technical regress varies across sectors. This can be imputed to different speeds of destruction of old techniques across sectors. These in turn can depend on several factors, namely the speed of technology transfer, the existing workers' skills and the managerial capabilities. In some sectors, new technologies can be adopted faster in all plants if both workers and managers have the "right" skills and capabilities and therefore creation will eventually counterbalance destruction with a limited technical regress observed in the sector. If a sector is more segmented, then it is possible that old techniques coexist with new techniques; therefore destruction offsets creation and therefore the sector can experience a considerable technical regress.

The estimated coefficients (in absolute value) of the z-variables are listed in the last rows of Table 3.7. It is important to notice that in the context of the Battese and Coelli (1995) model a negative (positive) sign of the DAR or ICR coefficient implies that firms with high DAR or ICR are more/less efficient. From these estimates, it is possible to see that both DAR and ICR influence positively efficiency in most sectors but the Extraction of Metals. In particular in

Table 3.7 Average marginal effects of measures of finance constraints by sector

Variable	Sector	Marginal effect
ICR	Extraction of metals	0.42
	Transformation of metals	0.28
	Food	1.17
	Tobacco	0.95
	Textiles	0.29
	Leather	0.0004
	Wood	0.04
	Paper	0.02
DAR	Extraction of metals	1.4
	Transformation of metals	0.1
	Food	0.0007
	Tobacco	0.54
	Textiles	0.29
	Leather	0.06
	Wood	0.09
	Paper	0.23

this sector, ICR affects positively technical efficiency while DAR does not. This result can be explained by reminding that firms in this sector can have access to external financial resources (thanks to government incentives) aimed in particular at the relaxing of the long-run constraint. So firms cannot really be considered debt-constrained and therefore tightening of the budget constraint cannot have an impact on efficiency. To test the significance of either DAR or ICR, I use the likelihood ratio testing procedure. The hypothesis test has been conducted with the unrestricted translog production function as the model under the null hypothesis. The likelihood ratio tests (in Table 3.6) show that both DAR and ICR are significant apart from the Tobacco sector.

The coefficients of either DAR or ICR do not tell directly the magnitude of the effect of changes in the DAR or ICR upon technical efficiency. Therefore, I have computed the partial derivatives of the technical efficiency predictor (or *marginal effects*) with respect to DAR first and ICR afterwards using the formula in Coelli (2003). They measure how reactive firms in the sector are in reducing their inefficiencies when there is a negative shock to their finances. The marginal effects are listed in Table 3.7. It is possible to see that, for instance, 1 per cent increase in DAR will increase the average technical efficiency score by 0.29 points in the Textiles sector. While in most sectors variations in finance constraints affect positively technical efficiency, it is interesting to notice that the size of the effect varies across sectors and within the same sector according to the whether the long-run or the short-run measure of finance constraints is considered. Consider the example of Food: a 1 per cent increase in ICR will increase efficiency by 1.17 points, while the same increase in DAR has a negligible impact on technical efficiency. This difference can be explained by looking at the composition of the sector. Small and medium-sized firms with scarce interest in expansion dominate the Food sector: these fund their activities mostly with internal resources and therefore they are very sensitive to changes in ICR. The same argument applies to the Leather sector but in the opposite direction: as larger firms with more cash-flow and more interest into expansion populate the sector, changes in ICR do not necessarily trigger an internal re-organization to release internal resources. However, the tightening of the long-run constraint may have an adverse impact on the potential expansion of firms and therefore start a process of technical inefficiency reduction.

3.5 Concluding remarks

In this chapter, I have argued that increases in financial pressure may be followed by positive changes in technical efficiency as firms will be induced to reduce some internal slack to offset the reduced availability of external financial resources. This is an application of the idea that financial constraints may have a direct influence on economic outcomes by affecting the ex-post distribution of rents among the agents that have contributed to generate them. This way, it is possible by increasing financial pressure to create the conditions for an increase in technical efficiency in spite of the fact the opposite is usually believed. In itself, this is not a bold proposition: indeed, as mentioned in Chapter 2, there already exists some empirical evidence suggesting a positive correlation between total factor productivity and increasing financial pressure (Nickell and Nicolitsas, 1999), although these previous papers have not clarified the exact mechanisms that underpin the empirical evidence. On the contrary, in this chapter, I have tried to identify theoretically the channels that allow increasing financial constraints to have a positive impact on productivity. More specifically, I make two hypotheses: first, I claim that increasing financial pressure aligns managers' interests with those of the firm's ownership; second, I assume that increases in productivity are due to reductions in technical inefficiency: as the firm cannot have access to additional resources to improve its technology (and therefore they do not experience technical change) it will try to improve the efficiency over time to improve productivity over time.

My starting point is the assumption that there exists an internal mechanism in the firm that generates the slack and so makes the firm appear technically inefficient. Therefore in the theoretical model, I consider a firm which is technically inefficient because of the mismatch of preferences between the managers and the ownership. Indeed, managers value leisure while the ownership is obviously interested in maximizing the firm's profits. As managers are paid only a fraction of their profits, this creates the potential for the hold-up problem where managers do not supply what would be the optimal effort from the standpoint of the ownership. My assumption is that this problem can only be mitigated when the external environment the firm operates in will change. So for instance changes in the financial position of the firm with the prospect of increasing financial pressure implies a reduction in the surplus generated by the firm and then a decrease of the share of surplus that managers can appropriate ex post. This mechanism may induce managers to re-align their incentives to those of the ownership with a reduction of the hold-up problem and then an increase of the firm's technical efficiency.

I have tested these predictions empirically by using a panel of 1,124 firms, covering the period 1989–1994 and belonging to the main eight sectors from Italian manufacturing. The results show that there is support for the hypothesis that technical efficiency may be affected by the availability of external financial resources; more precisely, once finance constraints get tighter, then firms experience an improvement in technical efficiency over time to guarantee gains in productivity and so positive increases in profits. One limitation of the empirical analysis is that I test a reduced form relationship between technical efficiency and financial pressure and therefore I cannot test whether the specific mechanism described in the theoretical model is at work in this sample of firms against alternative mechanisms. However, in spite of this, the empirical results are still of some value as they are a first step towards a more complete empirical analysis of the relationship between technical efficiency and credit constraints.

These results have interesting implications. Indeed, the notion that adverse financial shocks will negatively affect the firm does not always apply. This would be the case if the firm is efficient; however, firms will always have a certain degree of organizational slack that can be used to counterbalance the negative impact of adverse financial shocks. So in this respect, being technically inefficient is not necessarily bad for a firm: indeed, it may provide a cushion that buffers the impact of negative productivity shocks on firms. Of course this does not mean that increasing financial pressure may always have a beneficial impact on a firm. Indeed, it is important to recall that there are additional effects of financial constraints (as reviewed in Chapter 2) that can very easily offset their benefits (in terms of increased technical efficiency). Finally, these results suggest a potential non-linearity in the relationship between technical efficiency and financial constraints. Indeed, if a firm is relatively inefficient, then the impact of increasing financial pressure may be rather lenient as firms can absorb the negative shock by reducing technical efficiency. Less clear is the impact of an increase in the cost of external borrowing on firms that are on the frontier: as these do not have slack that can be used to reduce technical inefficiency, the impact on productivity is obviously not of the type predicted by the model. However, what it will be is open to speculations as the model contained in this chapter cannot predict what will happen in this case. This is therefore a point that warrants further investigation and that can therefore be left to future research.

Appendix

The Capitalia database (formerly known as the Mediocredito Centrale database) is one of the most valuable sources of information about Italian manufacturing available nowadays. The Capitalia surveys consider an open panel of Italian manufacturing firms, with about 4,500 firms for each survey. It was initiated in 1989 by the *Osservatorio delle piccole e medie imprese* with the declared purpose of collecting and disseminating information about the manufacturing world with a special emphasis on the small and medium-sized firms.[7] The database has been built and is continuously updated using a periodic survey administrated by the *Osservatorio delle piccole e medie imprese*. The survey belongs to the category of the so-called *mixed survey*; that is, the survey is sampling firms from 11 to 500 employees and it is exhaustive for firms with more than 500 employees. To construct the sample, the following sampling plan has been adopted: all firms with more than ten employees have been divided into homogeneous groups according to the variability of the *per capita* output. Then, from each group, a number of firms is selected proportionally. A supplementary list of about 8,000 firms has been constructed for each survey, in order to integrate by stratum the firms that had failed to reply. To ensure a good quality of the data, all the data collected from both the questionnaire and the balance sheets have been subject to a rigorous examination to detect eventual outliers. Emphasis has been given to the monitoring of the stratification variable; in this case, the number of firms within the sample has been compared with the actual number in each *strata*. When significant differences have been observed, there has been a re-sampling of the strata on the basis of the information drawn from the questionnaires.

Information is collected from two main sources: firms' balance sheets and a questionnaire, distributed periodically by the *Osservatorio delle piccole e medie imprese*. The questionnaire is divided into eight sections and collects information about the firm's internal organization, its prevailing economic activity, the previous education of employees, the amount of investment in R&D and the links with foreign markets.[8] It also provides qualitative information ranging from general aspects (year when the firm was founded, legal form, reorganizations, ownership and control, groups and consortia) to firms' finance and financial and fiscal incentives. Most of this qualitative information relates to the three-year period as a whole with only a small subset of information being available for each year. The balance sheets contain quantitative information relating to the firms' main financial indicators for each of the three years under consideration in each wave of the survey. The number of firms replying to the questionnaire is different from the number of firms providing the balance sheets: indeed, 4,431 firms have returned the questionnaire in 1994, while 2,519 firms have provided information about their balance sheets for the period 1989–1994.

Given the amount of the collected information, the Capitalia database allows a researcher to get a more complete overview of the Italian manufacturing world than similar databases (like the ones from *Mediobanca* and from the *Centrale dei Bilanci*). To extract the data-sets, I have used the information contained in the 5th and 6th Surveys, published by the *Osservatorio* in 1997. Our data refer to the report published in 1992 that presented data relative to 4123 firms from 1989 to 1991. The second report was published in 1997 and collected the balance sheets of 2,519 firms from 1992 to 1994 and the replies to the questionnaire of 4,431 firms relative to 1994. However, the information from the balance sheets has been made homogeneous so that it is possible to have the balance sheets of 2,519 firms from 1989 to 1994. More specifically, to build up the employed panel data-sets, I have used only the information provided from the balance sheets in the last published report to get an homogeneous data-set.

4 Product market competition, financial pressure and producers' cooperatives

4.1 Introduction

In the previous chapter it has been established that the tightening of financial constraints may induce firms to reduce their technical inefficiency (rather than cutting the level of production or the demand for investment) when technical inefficiency arises from the mismatch between the managers' preferences and those of the ownership. In this case, managers may want to increase their effort if they anticipate that the increase in the financial pressure will hit negatively their financial bonus from the firm. So in a sense, financial pressure acts as a disciplining force that helps to align the interests of the management to those of the ownership. Now, economic theory has pointed out that financial pressure is not the only mechanism that can exert a positive effect on technical efficiency; for instance, increasing product market competition may produce the same results. Both Vickers (1995) and Nickell (1996) have identified two channels through which competition may induce conventional firms to be more efficient. The first effect is called "discovery and selection". In a model of entry with Cournot competition, a low-cost entrant may drive some high-cost incumbent out of the market and the profitability of firms will be affected as output shifts from high-cost firms to low-cost firms (Vickers, 1995). The second effect of competition is that of sharpening incentives for managers, as they try to compensate the decreasing market share with higher productivity (Nickell, 1996). Indeed, in the presence of increasing product market competition managers anticipate that the rents they earn may decrease and may decide to increase effort so that the fall of the organizational slack may offset the fall of the managerial rents.

Not surprisingly, some authors have tried to establish whether these two mechanisms (state of competition in the product market and financial pressure) are substitutes or complementary to each other or (in other words) the extent to which they reinforce or offset each other (Nickell *et al.*, 1997; Aghion *et al.*, 2003). It is usually believed that they are complementary as it is usually assumed that the main channels through which they exert a positive impact on firms' productivity is by reducing organizational slack; so in this case firms with a higher debt repayment obligation will try to improve their technical efficiency or productivity, in general, if the competitive pressure is increasing (Aghion and

Griffith, 2005). Therefore, in this case the net impact on technical efficiency of jointly increasing product market competition and financial pressure has to be positive. However, the empirical evidence on this point is rather ambiguous. Indeed, empirically increasing competition appears to increase productivity levels in firms with low debt pressure. Nickell *et al.* (1997) have looked at the joint impact of financial pressure and product market competition on productivity growth in a data-set of British firms and have found that as financial pressure increases, the impact of competition decreases; in other words they are substitute. Also, there is no evidence of a positive interaction between increasing product market competition and financial pressure in fostering productivity growth. Indeed, Aghion *et al.* (2003) have considered the joint impact of financial pressure and competition on patent counts (a measure of firms' innovation) in a data-set of British firms listed on the London Stock Exchange Market. They have identified the firms facing the highest financial pressure in order to consider whether the impact of competition differs for them relative to the whole sample of firms. Their results suggest that financial pressure and competition are neither complementary nor substitutes in order to increase firms' productivity. Overall, these results have cast some doubts on the extent to which slack reduction is the main channel through which increasing competition and increasing financial pressure can jointly enhance productivity (both in growth and in level). However, these mixed results may be explained by recalling that theoretically the complementarities between financial pressure and product market competition rely on the assumption that the firms' managers have a preference for a high level of slack. Now it is possible that these firms in the sample are too heterogeneous to satisfy this theoretical requirement (in other words, their managers might have a preference for a low level of slack).

In this chapter I consider again the relationship among technical efficiency, product market competition and financial pressure but, unlike the previous literature, I focus on the producers' cooperatives. The reasons for this choice can be outlined as follows. Cooperatives tend to be a rather homogeneous type of firm where for organizational reasons there is an immediate link between workers' share of surplus and the co-op's performance. Indeed, workers (whether members or not of the cooperative) receive a profit-sharing bonus that is a direct function of the firm's profits (Perotin and Robinson, 1998). Also cooperatives have been subject in recent years to a substantial increase in the level of product market competition they face (Birgegaard and Genberg, 1994; Filippi, 2004). The increasing integration of what were once national product markets implies that even co-ops (traditionally operating in niche segments of national markets) have to face increasing competitive pressure from foreign firms, as it happens with conventional firms (Maietta and Sena, 2007). At the same time, it is well known that cooperatives are traditionally subject to substantial financial constraints (Hailu *et al.*, 2007) and therefore this makes them a very interesting case-study to analyse how these two forces (state of competition in the product market and increasing financial pressure) interact with each other and how they jointly affect technical efficiency.

In some sense this is not very different from asking (a) whether co-ops are more or less efficient than conventional firms, and (b) what are the determinants of these efficiency differentials. Now it is a contentious issue in the economic literature whether cooperatives tend to be more (or at least as) efficient than (as) conventional firms (Porter and Scully, 1987; Bonin *et al.*, 1993). From a theoretical standpoint, there are a number of reasons why a cooperative should experience a higher level of efficiency than a conventional firm. A first group of theories emphasizes the positive impact that profit sharing can have on workers' effort (Uvalic, 1991; Weitzman, 1995; Blair, 1995, 1999; Cahuc and Dormont, 1997). In a conventional firm, asymmetric information does not allow the management to verify the workers' effort and so workers may prefer to shirk and so exert the less than optimal level of effort. The profit-sharing agreement existing in a cooperative may help to realign the workers' incentives to those of the firm in several ways. It may enhance workers' effort in return for what they could perceive as the company's fairness in letting them participate in the economic success of the firm (so-called gift exchange) (Sessions, 1992). Profit sharing may also provide employees in a cooperative with an incentive to monitor each other and put pressure on shirkers (Jones and Svejnar, 1982). Finally, it may give workers and managers the incentive to circulate information, which in turn may limit the asymmetric information problem and so increase the productivity (Cable and Wilson, 1990). A second group of theories looks at the role that profit sharing in a cooperative can have on the workforce attributes, for instance skill levels. It is well known that in conventional firms workers may not be willing to invest in firm-specific skills. The reasons for this are well articulated in Hart (1995). When the workers' investment is not contractible (i.e. contracts are incomplete) and, at the same time, workers have to bear all the costs of the investment, they may correctly anticipate that the firm will try to expropriate them after the investment has been made. Therefore, they find it optimal to under-invest. Profit sharing can, however, help to solve this problem. Indeed, with profit sharing workers are made residual claimants of the firm, as they are entitled to a portion of the profits. In this case, workers, aware of the fact that some of the improved performance will accrue to them, will be willing to invest in costly firm-specific skills as profit-sharing reduces the potential for ex-post expropriation.

As the above-mentioned literature, the purpose of this chapter is to understand what factors may explain the fact that cooperatives tend to be more efficient than conventional firms. However, it differs from the previous literature in that I focus on the role that the state of competition in the product market and the financial pressure can jointly play to improve the co-ops' technical efficiency. A certain number of papers have analysed the possibility that co-ops' efficiency can be affected either by the state of competition in the product market or by the financial pressure the co-op is exposed to (see Maietta and Sena, 2004, 2007; Hailu *et al.* 2007). In both cases, the mechanisms through which either increasing competition or increasing financial pressure can independently have a positive impact on co-ops' efficiency are well established: consider a cooperative where workers (a) have control rights over a specific "asset", their effort and, (b) are paid by a fixed fraction of the overall surplus. The cooperative organizing the production uses both capital and the workers' effort as inputs. To be able to produce, the cooperative needs the workers' effort: that is, without the workers' effort, production cannot start. I assume there is a lag between the time the firm starts the production and the time the workers decide on effort, and therefore, because of this, a standard hold-up problem arises (Hart, 1995). Workers supply the amount of effort that maximizes their own expected pay-off from the relationship with the firm, instead of the overall surplus (that is, both the workers' and the co-op's surplus). Therefore, the supplied effort is sub-optimal from the firm's standpoint and so it will be technically inefficient, as the actual output will be lower than the potential output (or the output produced by the other firms in the industry). Suppose now there is an increase in the competition faced by the cooperative in the market. This may be due to several factors, some of which are related to economic policy (like the reduction of tariffs and other artificially created barriers to entry) and some to consumers' tastes. From the workers' standpoint, this implies that their profit-sharing bonus decreases as well and therefore they may want to readjust their effort so to counterbalance the effect of the negative shock on the profit-sharing bonus. However, this will not have any impact on the profit-sharing bonus at this stage (as the level of effort is decided in the period before the shock) but it will have an effect on the next period's bonus. These re-adjustments affect the firm's technical efficiency. As workers increase their investment, the actual output increases and gets closer to the potential output. The result is that inefficiency for the firm reduces over time. The mechanism is not very different when the impact of financial pressure on a cooperative's technical efficiency is considered. Workers of a cooperative receive a financial bonus that is proportional to the co-op's realized profits; obviously if they anticipate the possibility that the bonus can decrease following an increase in the financial pressure, they will increase their effort and reduce the internal inefficiencies in the co-op. Also, the model predicts that as financial pressure increases then the impact of increasing product market competition on technical efficiency will be larger than an absence of financial pressure. So the model provides two hypotheses to test: the first one is that increases in the financial pressure are followed by increases in technical efficiency. The second one is that competition and financial pressure can jointly increase technical efficiency. The first hypothesis will be tested by estimating a reduced form model where measures of technical efficiency (calculated by using Data Envelopment Analysis – DEA) are regressed on indicators of financial constraints (as already done in the previous chapter). Afterwards, I test empirically the extent to which financial pressure and state of competition in the product market are substitutes or complementary in a panel of Italian cooperative firms, specializing in the production of wine, over the time 1996–2001. This will be done by estimating a one-stage stochastic production frontier where measures of technical efficiency are computed conditional on a set of factors (in this case, state of competition in the product market and financial pressure) that can explain the distribution of scores across firms (Battese and Coelli, 1995). Stochastic frontiers have been widely used in the comparative economics literature and the literature on workers' participation to compare the effects of different types of ownership on technical efficiency (Ferrantino *et al.*, 1995; Mosheim, 2002). This methodology offers the advantage that it allows us to compute the firms' technical efficiency while at the same time controlling for the factors that can affect the dispersion of efficiency across the firms. The choice of Italy is due to the fact that this country has got a very large cooperative sector and indeed, not surprisingly, several studies have been conducted on Italian cooperatives with the purpose of testing several hypotheses of the literature on co-ops (Jones and Svejnar, 1985; Bartlett *et al.*, 1992).

The structure of the chapter is the following. Section 4.2 formalizes in a simple partial equilibrium model the relationship between competition, technical efficiency and financial pressure in a producer's co-op. The empirical model and the results are presented in Section 4.3. Finally, some concluding remarks are offered in Section 4.4.

4.2 The general framework

Consider an industry with $i = 1, \ldots,$ N firms. These include both conventional firms and producers' co-ops. Both types of productive unit can hire one worker from a pool of workers of homogeneous quality. The allocation of each worker to each firm is pre-determined and the worker cannot leave the firm. Each firm produces a differentiated good and faces a downward-sloping demand curve. Both the conventional firm and the co-op use the same type of production technology, where both workers' effort and capital appear as inputs:

$$y_{i,t} = \bar{k}_{i,t-1}^{1-\alpha} e_{i,t-1}^{\alpha},$$
(4.1)

with $\alpha < 1$. In each firm, workers have to make the effort of learning new techniques every period; these will be used though in the next period. This implies that the decision of how much effort to devote to the firm is made in period t–1 and that it cannot be undone. I assume that these are specific to the firm and so they cannot be used in another firm. This assumption is not as far-fetched as it may appear: for instance, in agricultural firms techniques for the production of wine are firm-specific as they vary across firms according to the quality of land and so on. As in the previous chapter, I assume that some firms (either co-ops or conventional firms) face finance constraints that may due to the existence of asymmetric information in the credit market. This implies that the firm has to use less capital than really needed and therefore as in the previous chapter, the existence of financial constraints implies that $k_{i,t-1} = \bar{k}_{i,t-1}$.

The demand function for the output of both the co-op and the conventional firm is the same and is expressed by the following equation:

$$p_{i,t} = y_{i,t}^{\theta-1} \bar{y}_{i,t}^{1-\theta} = y_{i,t}^{\theta-1},$$
(4.2)

where $y_{i,t}$ is the good produced by firm i, y is an index of the overall market demand, assumed for simplicity to be equal to 1 and $0 < \theta < 1$. Consistently with the previous literature, θ is an indicator of product market competition, where a large value is an indication that product market competition is intense. Many different factors, some related to specific policies and some to consumers' taste, affect the intensity of competition in the product market. Among the policy-related factors we find tariffs and other artificially created barriers to entry that reduce competition, as well as policies that advance competition by introducing product standardization. Among the taste-related factors, I notice that firms can avoid competition by exploiting the fact that consumers typically may have a preference for a particular variety of brands.

The main difference between the co-ops and the conventional firms is that the former reward their workers with a share s_i of the profit $p_{i,t}y_i$. Indeed, it is common practice in Italian producers' co-ops that workers receive additional bonus payments that depend on the level of the profits. Here I capture this fact by assuming that the financial reward is related to the profits, and for simplicity I assume that the wage is equal to this financial reward. The per period utility function of the worker is defined as:

$$U_{i,t} = c_{i,t} - \frac{1}{2}e_{i,t}^2, \tag{4.3}$$

with $c_{i,t}$ being the consumption of the worker employed in the firm i at time t. The budget constraint for workers in a co-op is $c_{i,t} = s_i p_{i,t} y_i$. Lifetime utility is then:

$$U_i = \sum_{t=0}^{T} \delta^t (s_i p_{i,t} y_{i,t} - \frac{1}{2}e_{i,t}^2), \tag{4.4}$$

where δ is the discount factor and $e - 1 = 0$.

From now on, I focus on the co-op's case and I derive the expression for the co-op's technical efficiency by backward induction. Therefore, the timeline of the model is as follows. At time 0, the co-op is set up and the worker is hired. At time 1, the worker decides on e. At time 2, capital is bought and so production can take place. Output is then sold and the surplus shared between the worker and the co-op's owners. The worker consumes at the end of the period. Also in this case (as in the previous chapter), the hold-up problem can arise: the difference now is that it is the worker who is involved in it (rather than the manager as in the previous chapter), as he maximizes his own expected pay-off from the relationship with the co-op, instead of the overall surplus (that is, both the worker's and co-op's surplus). Therefore, the effort is optimal from the worker's standpoint, but not for the co-op. For this reason, the co-op's actual output will differ from the output it could potentially produce if there was no hold-up problem and so it will appear technically inefficient. In period 2, the worker is not going to supply any effort (as there is no future) and now production takes place:

$$y_{i,2} = \bar{k}_{i,1}^{1-\alpha} e_{i,1}^{\alpha} \qquad (4.5)$$

and the worker's profit-sharing bonus (that is consumed by the worker) is $s_{i,2} y_{1,2}$. In period 1, the worker's effort choice is:

$$e_{i,1}^* = \arg\max \delta s_i p_{i,2} y_{i,2} - \frac{1}{2} e_{i,1}^2 \qquad (4.6)$$

$$= (\bar{k}_{i,1}^{\theta(1-\alpha)} \delta s_i \theta \alpha)^{\frac{1}{1-\theta(\alpha-1)}} \qquad (4.7)$$

In period 0, the worker faces a similar problem and he chooses similarly. Effort is increasing in the degree of competition (θ) and decreasing in the measure of financial constraint.

Proposition 1. An unexpected increase in product market competition induces an increase of the worker's effort. The same goes for an unexpected increase in the financial pressure.

Proof. Compute the derivative of the optimal effort with respect to θ:

$$\frac{\partial e_{i,1}^*}{\partial \theta} = \frac{1}{1-\theta\alpha+\theta} [-\ln\theta + \frac{1}{\theta} - \ln(\alpha\delta s_i)] + \frac{1-\alpha}{(1-\theta\alpha+\theta)^2} \ln \bar{k}_{i,t-1} > 0. \qquad (4.8)$$

Also the second derivative of (4.8) with respect to the measure of financial constraint will be positive as well:

$$\frac{\partial e_{i,1}^*}{\partial\theta\partial\bar{k}} = \frac{1-\alpha}{(1-\theta\alpha+\theta)^2} \ln \bar{k}_{i,t-1} > 0. \qquad (4.9)$$

Consider now a relaxation of the financial constraint that induces an increase of the stock of capital available to the co-op for production. In this case:

$$\frac{\partial e_{i,1}^*}{\partial \bar{k}_{i,1}} = [\alpha\theta\delta s_i]^{\frac{1}{1-\theta(\alpha-1)}} \frac{\theta(1-\alpha)}{1-\theta(\alpha-1)} \bar{k}^{\frac{\theta(1-\alpha)-1+\theta(\alpha-1)}{1-\theta(\alpha-1)}} < 0. \qquad (4.10)$$

The reasons for these results are no different from the ones I have considered in the previous chapter. The worker makes his effort decision based on his expectations about future revenues. If he anticipates that either competition gets stiffer or financial pressure increases and that therefore his expected profit-sharing bonus will decrease, he decides to spend more effort so to increase the firm's output and this way his profit-sharing bonus. Also, the impact of increasing product market competition on effort will be larger, the higher the financial pressure as the worker anticipates these two forces will jointly affect adversely the profit-sharing bonus and he will try to offset them by increasing his effort.

I can measure technical efficiency in firm i in period t as the ratio between the actual level of output produced at time t by the firm i ($y_{i,t}$), and the output of the best-practice firm, which could be produced at time t ($\hat{y}_{i,t}$) (Farrell, 1957). The best-practice firm may be either a co-op or a conventional firm:

$$TE_{i,t} = \frac{y_{i,t}}{\hat{y}_{i,t}}. \tag{4.11}$$

My main interest is to find out how technical efficiency in periods 1 and 2 in firm i is affected by either a permanent, but unexpected, change in the product market competition in period 1 or a permanent, but unexpected, change in the financial pressure the co-op faces. The fact that it is unexpected implies that it could not be taken into account when effort was decided in period 0. The fact that it is permanent implies that the worker will wish to adjust the effort choice made in period 1, once he has observed the change in period 1. It is also import-ant to note that both shocks are assumed to be specific to firm i. Therefore, I can take the potential output as given.

Consider first what happens to technical efficiency in period 1. Since the effort has already been decided in period 0 based on expected competition and financial pressure, I get:

$$\frac{\partial TE_{i,1}}{\partial \theta} = 0. \tag{4.12}$$

Next, consider period 2. After the change has been observed in period 1, it is incorporated in the expectations and the worker adjusts the effort choice to accommodate the new environment in period 2. The change in technical effi-ciency in period 2 following a change in product market competition is:

$$\frac{\partial TE_{i,2}}{\partial \theta} = \frac{\alpha(\partial e_{i,1}^{*}/\partial \theta)^{\alpha-1} \bar{k}_{i,1}^{1-\alpha}}{\bar{k}_{i,1}^{1-\alpha} \hat{e}_{i,1}^{\alpha}} > 0. \tag{4.13}$$

The intuition behind this result is quite simple. I know from above that the worker may want to readjust his effort so to counterbalance the negative effect of competition. Also, the decision of increasing effort will only have an impact on the next period's profit-sharing bonus because of the time lag between the workers' decision on effort and production. These re-adjustments have an impact on the co-op's technical efficiency. As workers increase their effort in the first period, the actual output in period 2 increases and gets closer to the potential output. The result is that inefficiency in period 2 for the co-op reduces.

Consider now the impact of a change in the financial pressure the firm is facing:

$$\frac{\partial TE_{i,2}}{\partial \bar{k}} = \frac{(1-\alpha)(\partial e_{i,1}^{*}/\partial \bar{k})^{-\alpha} e_{i,1}^{\alpha}}{\bar{k}_{i,1}^{1-\alpha} \hat{e}_{i,1}^{\alpha}} < 0. \tag{4.14}$$

This result is not surprising. As credit constraints get less binding for the co-op, the workers are less willing to put more effort in the co-op and this has an adverse impact on its technical efficiency. On the other side, this implies that technical efficiency increases as financial constraints get tighter.

Finally, do financial pressure and product market competition work as complement or substitute mechanisms to improve a co-op's technical efficiency? Consider (4.13) and compute the second derivative with respect to the financial constraint. The sign is again positive as long as there are increasing returns to scale:

$$\frac{\partial TE_{i,2}}{\partial \theta \partial \bar{k}} = \frac{\alpha(\alpha-1)(\partial e_{i,1}^{*}/\partial \theta \partial \bar{k})^{\alpha-2}}{\hat{e}_{i,1}^{\alpha}} > 0. \tag{4.15}$$

In other words, the impact of increasing product market competition on technical efficiency will be larger in the presence of high debt pressure as long as the impact of an increase in effort on the level of production is quite large. This is not surprising: the impact on effort must be of such magnitude that it has to offset the impact of both increasing financial pressure and product market competition on efficiency.

4.3 The empirical analysis

4.3.1 The institutional framework

The Italian cooperative system is one of the largest in the Western economies and several studies have been conducted on Italian producers and workers' cooperatives (Bartlett *et al.*, 1992; Jones and Svejnar, 1985). The Italian cooperative movement goes back to the insurance societies of the nineteenth century with a first confederation of cooperatives (Lega Nazionale delle Cooperative) established in 1886 (Pencavel *et al.*, 2005). Today, the cooperative sector is quite large and contributes to the 7–8 per cent of GDP (Lega delle Cooperative, 2006).

Italian co-ops operate on the principles of the International Cooperative Alliance: one-member-one-vote, free and voluntary membership and limited remuneration of the underwritten capital. Members of a co-op provide a portion of its capital with the agreement that on leaving they will be repaid the value of the contributed capital. Twenty per cent of a co-op's revenues is allocated to the legal reserve fund that is collectively owned and cannot be recouped by individual workers upon leaving the firm. The remaining profits can be used for remunerating capital underwritten by members, to increase the reserve fund, to finance social and service activities and for distributing among the workers/members in proportion to their work. Co-ops can hire workers who are not required to be members even if it is quite common for these to become members of the co-op (Pencavel *et al.*, 2006). Most co-ops distribute profits to members and non-members on the same terms, but there may be bonuses that members enjoy. The main decision-making body is the General Assembly. By vote, the General Assembly selects a Council, the principal supervisory body that appoints the managers and specifies the general policies. Typically, though, there is extensive participation by co-op members in decision-making and considerable turnover of officers.

4.3.2 The empirical specification

The key predictions from the model are two: (1) increasing competition and financial pressure are complementary mechanisms to improve co-ops' technical efficiency, and (2) increases in financial pressure are followed by increases in technical efficiency. To test the first prediction, I use the so-called frontier approach to the measurement of technical efficiency where technical efficiency scores are computed as the distance from an estimated parametric production frontier. More specifically, I use the model by Battese and Coelli (1995) where the inefficiency effects (u_{it}) are expressed as an explicit function of a vector of firm-specific variables and a random error. The advantage of this approach is that the technology and the inefficiency parameters are so obtained by using a single-stage estimation procedure and so it is possible to simultaneously compute efficiency scores while controlling for the factors which influence the distribution of scores across different observations. The model specification is the following:

$$\ln(y_{it}) = \beta 0 + \beta 1 \ln(K_{it}) + \beta 2 l n(M_{it}) + \beta 3 \ln(L_{it}) + \beta 4 \ln(K_{it})2 + \beta 5 l n(M_{it})2 + \beta 6 \ln(L_{it})2 + \beta 7 l n(K_{it})\ln(M_{it}) + \beta 8 \ln(K_{it})\ln(L_{it}) + \beta 9 \ln(L_{it})\ln(M_{it}) + \rho 10 \text{ YEAR} + (v_{it} - u_{it}), i = 1, \ldots, N, t = 1, \ldots, T, \quad (4.16)$$

where $\ln(y_{it})$ is the logarithm of the production of the i-th firm at the t-th time period, $\ln(K_{it})$, $\ln(L_{it})$, $\ln(M_{it})$ are the logs of capital, labour and material, respectively, of the i-th firm at the t-th time period and β is a vector of unknown parameters. I allow for the possibility of disembodied technical progress by introducing a time trend (YEAR) in the model. The v_{it} are random variables which are assumed to be iid as a $N(0,\sigma v2)$, and independent of the u_{it}; in turn, these are non-negative random variables assumed to account for technical inefficiency in production and to be independently distributed as truncations at zero of the $N(\mu_{it},\sigma u2)$ distribution with $\mu_{it} = z_{it}\delta$, where z_{it} is a p × 1 vector of variables which may influence the efficiency of a firm and δ is a 1 × p vector of parameters to be estimated together with $\sigma2 = \sigma v2 + \sigma u2$ and $\gamma = \sigma u2/(\sigma v2 + \sigma u2)$. Our efficiency effects model is the following:

$$u_{it} = \delta o + \delta1\ SOUTH + \delta3\ YEAR + \delta4\ COMP_{i,t-1} + \delta6\ DARi,t - 1 +$$
$$\delta7\ DARi,t - 1*COMP_{i,t-1}$$

where SOUTH is the dummy variable for firms located in the south of Italy, COOP is the dummy for the co-ops, YEAR is the time trend and COMP is the measure of the firm's market power. This is measured by the lagged value of the individual firm's market share; the market share has been lagged so to avoid potential endogeneity problems in the regression model (Amemiya and Macurdy, 1986; Hausman, 1978; Nakamura and Nakamura, 1981; Greene, 1993; Wu, 1973, 1974).[1] I expect this variable to have a positive impact on co-ops' efficiency. As in the previous chapter, financial pressure is measured by the Debt to Asset Ratio (DAR). Again my expectation is that this variable has a positive impact on the co-ops' efficiency. I also control for the firm's location with the variable SOUTH in the specification of the inefficiency model. It is a well-established piece of evidence in the Italian literature that location matters for productive efficiency. For instance, southern firms tend to be more inefficient because of the existence of local factors such as infrastructure endowment, external economies linked to the local technological potential or level of indus-trialization, the presence of organized crime, and so on. In this study I do not attempt to measure the impact of those factors separately. Rather, I control for them, using a dummy variable related to the geographic location of the firm; following common practice, I divide Italy in north-centre and south. Among the regressors, I also introduce the time trend to control for yearly variability due to phenomena such as the impact of weather, pests and others on the vineyards and then on the wine quantity (INEA, 2001).

To test the second hypothesis, I use Data Envelopment Analysis (DEA).[2] DEA does not require an explicit functional form and constructs the produc-tion frontier (with respect to which a firm's efficiency is measured) from the observed input–output ratios by linear programming techniques. Appendix D contains additional details on the DEA maximization problem. In this case, the distinctive advantage of the non-parametric approach is that, by not requiring a specific functional form for the production process, it allows us to accommodate different functional relationships consistently with the theo-retical model. In my specification, I have applied an output-oriented Data Envelopment Analysis with variable returns to scale (Banker *et al.*, 1984) to each cross-section of firms and repeated for each year in our sample. DEA is done jointly in each year for cooperatives, since they are homogeneous in the technology they use, as it is customarily assumed in the literature (see, for example, Ferrier and Valdmanis, 1996). Afterwards, I regress the technical efficiency change indexes on DAR, after controlling for eventual environ-mental variables affecting the change in technical efficiency. I expect the coefficients of this variable to be positive and significant, so implying that a restriction of financial resources affects positively the co-ops' technical efficiency change.

4.3.3 The empirical analysis: data and descriptive statistics

The data set I use is an unbalanced panel of Italian conventional and cooperative firms from 1996 to 2001, belonging to the sector of Wine Production[3] (corresponding to the code A01131 of the Ateco 91 classification supplied by ISTAT, Italian Statistical Office). The data-set has been extracted from AIDA,[4] a database collecting the annual balance sheets of those Italian companies whose operating revenue is equal to a minimum of €1 million. In addition to the information contained in the annual reports, the database reports information on companies' location, the legal status and additional financial data, like short-term and long-term debts. The total number of observations over the five years is 413. According to their legal status, 63 firms (corresponding to 250 observations over the whole time period) are cooperatives.

The wine industry has been selected for a number of reasons: first the firms' output mix is limited compared to that of firms belonging to other sectors as they produce only wine;[5] therefore the firms in our sample will be more homogeneous in terms of technology. Homogeneity of the technology available to the firms in the data-set under consideration is an important requirement of the frontier analysis to be able to get meaningful frontier estimates. In addition, the number of cooperatives in the Italian wine industry has always been substantial and this implies that their market share has always been quite comparable to that of the conventional firms (Van Djik and Mackel, 1991; van Bekkum and van Dijk, 1998).[6] Finally, firms operating in the wine sector require workers to have some firm-specific skills, consistent with what is described in the theoretical model. Indeed, the land and weather conditions are different from firm to firm and this implies that the workers are required to learn skills (Pagano, 1992; Huffman, 2001) that cannot be easily transferred to other firms even if they operate in the same sector (Lombardi and Mele, 1993; Galizzi, 2000). Human capital in agriculture is highly location-specific and so firm-specific because land and weather conditions are different from place to place and their knowledge influences workers' productivity (Pagano, 1992). The same can be said for the production of wine, derived from the processing of grapes.

In the production set, output is measured by the company's sales plus the change in inventories deflated by the appropriate production index (ISTAT, 2002). Among the inputs, I include the intermediate consumption (as a measure of the raw materials), the capital and the labour. Intermediate consumption is defined as the sum of materials and services while capital is the sum (at book value) of land, buildings, machinery and other fixed assets. Both variables have been deflated by the price index of material consumption and of investment goods for the beverage industry, respectively (ISTAT, 2002). All these variables (both of output and inputs) are expressed in 1995 million Italian liras. Labour is the number of employees at the end of the fiscal year and includes both full-time

Table 4.1 Descriptive statistics

Statistics	Output*	Capital*	Inter. consum.*	Labour	Market share**	DAR
Cooperatives						
1997	8,852	3,188	7,784	27	1.46	0.71
1998	7,181	2,918	6,308	22	1.02	0.7
1999	7,456	2,990	6,575	21	1.05	0.7
2000	8,979	3,715	7,896	25	1.03	0.7
2001	7,359	3,653	6,409	23	0.84	0.68

Notes
* 1995 ml Italian liras.
** percentage.

and seasonal workers. The market share has been computed as the firm's total output over the industry total output (Klinedinst *et al.*, 1998). As in the previous chapter, we measure the financial pressure by the Debt to Asset Ratio (DAR) of each unit.

Table 4.1 reports the sample statistics for the output, inputs, market share and debt to asset ratio (DAR) for the cooperative firms, respectively.

On average, cooperatives produce more than conventional firms, use less capital and labour but have more intermediate consumption than conventional firms for each year under consideration. The stiffening of the competitive environment is reflected in the steady decline of the market share over the period for both types of firms. This is the result of two simultaneous factors: first, the market share of Italian wines in foreign markets has decreased due to aggressive marketing of foreign wine producers in the international markets. Second, during this same period, the European Union (EU) has started to reduce the size of subsidies to firms operating in the agricultural sector and this has implied a downsizing of most companies whose size was not financially viable (van Bekkum and van Dijk, 1998). Interestingly, though, in spite of the general decrease of market share across the two groups of firms, the co-ops still have been able to keep a larger market share than traditional firms. Finally, the DAR appears to be rather high, showing relatively high levels of debt; however, this does appear to vary too much over time.

4.3.4 The results

The Maximum Likelihood estimates of (4.16) are reported in Table 4.2.

The LR test on γ (Ho: $\gamma = 0$) is equal to with number of restrictions equal to 7 (against a critical value of 7.05 at a 5 per cent significance level);[7] this shows that the frontier model is a significant improvement over the traditional OLS estimation of the production function. The translog specification has also been tested against the Cobb–Douglas specification and is accepted on the basis of a LR test that is equal to 254.15 with number of restrictions equal to 6 (against a critical value of 12.6 at a 5 per cent significance level). The significance of

Table 4.2 MLE estimates

Variable	Coefficient	S.E.	t-ratio
Constant	−0.030	0.008	−3.729
LnK	0.025	0.009	2.822
LnM	0.875	0.010	83.382
LnL	0.064	0.008	8.036
LnK^2	0.005	0.004	1.347
LnM^2	0.088	0.006	14.476
LnL^2	0.026	0.008	3.220
LnK*LnM	−0.043	0.008	−5.237
LnK*LnL	−0.007	0.009	−0.713
LnL*LM	−0.052	0.008	−6.244
YEAR	0.010	0.012	0.903
SOUTH	0.005	0.002	2.431
Inefficiency model parameters			
μ_0	0.788	0.127	−6.213
YEAR	0.0004	0.0002	2.021
SOUTH	−0.166	0.103	−1.610
COMP	−0.795	0.098	−8.127
DAR	−0.031	0.009	−3.426
DAR*COMP	0.00003	0.0003	0.097
σ^2	0.019	0.003	6.211
γ	0.860	0.036	23.819

the coefficients related to inputs is generally quite good; there is no empirical evidence of disembodied technical progress.[8] On average for the co-ops, the values of input elasticities are respectively equal to: 0.024 for capital, 0.875 for intermediate consumption and 0.06 for labour. Returns to scale tend to be constant. The dummy for the south of Italy is significant: firms located there tend to use a different technology. Among the factors used to explain inefficiency, the coefficient of the variable YEAR is statistically significant, while the dummy for the south is not. The competition variable is statistically significant and negative: generally competition does have a positive impact on efficiency; the same result is obtained for the DAR. This result for co-ops is in line with our theoretical expectation. The interaction term between product market competition and the DAR is positive but it is not significant. This implies that increasing product market competition and DAR do work as complementary instruments in our sample but it is not clear whether this relationship still holds in the population.

Finally, from Table 4.3 it is possible to observe that technical efficiency has increased for the co-ops in the period under consideration.

Interestingly, conventional firms have experienced decreasing levels of efficiency over the same period of time. These results are not in contrast with the findings from previous studies on Italian cooperatives. Jones and Svejnar (1985) find that the superior performance of Italian producers' cooperatives could be ascribed to structural characteristics of co-ops like profit-sharing and participation. Also,

Table 4.3 Technical efficiency estimates

Year	Cooperatives
1997	0 .957
1998	0.963
1999	0.967
2000	0.964
2001	0.960
Mean	0.962

Table 4.4 Average level of *output-oriented* technical efficiency

Aggregate	Technical efficiency
Cooperatives	
1996	0.868
1997	0.789
1998	0.859
1999	0.880
2000	0.818
2001	0.882

Bartlett *et al.* (1992) find that Italian co-ops achieve higher levels of both labour and capital productivity than comparable private firms.

The yearly average level of the *output-oriented* measure of technical efficiency for co-ops is reported in Table 4.4.

The average level of technical efficiency is quite high with marked annual differences. Cooperatives' efficiency decreases in 1997 and 2000. Afterwards, I test whether financial pressure has any impact on the variation of technical efficiency over time. To this purpose, I regress the technical efficiency change indexes on DAR, after controlling for eventual environmental variables affecting the change in technical efficiency. I expect the coefficients of this variable to be positive and significant for the cooperatives, implying that a restriction of financial resources affects positively a co-op's technical efficiency change. Table 4.5 reports the results of the second-stage analysis.

Since the panel is not balanced, it was not possible to derive five indexes of technical efficiency change for all firms (Balestra and Nerlove, 1966; Chamberlain, 1982); however, the number of observations is still high for both the regressions. Following common practice in these contexts, a log-linear functional form has been adopted. As a test of serial correlation among the residuals, we have used the F-version of the Lagrange multiplier test for first-order (or second-order) residual serial correlation in panel data (Baltagi, 2001). In any case, the t-ratios of the regression coefficients are always derived from variance–covariance matrices adjusted for heteroskedasticity and serial correlation through the Newey–West procedure. The fit of the regressions is more than

Table 4.5 OLS second-stage estimates for cooperatives

Variable	Coefficient	t-statistics	p-value
Constant	−0.04	−1.15	0.25
Y99	−0.02	−1.07	0.29
Y00	−0.13	−6.19	0.00
Y01	−0.02	−0.92	0.36
South	0.01	0.51	0.61
Log[TE(−1)]	−0.56	−8.33	0.00
Log[TE(−2)]	0.27	4.17	0.00
Log[DAR(−1)]	0.06	1.99	0.05
Adjusted R^2	0.48		
LM statistic − (1st order)	1.93		0.17
LM statistic − (2nd order)	2.83		0.07
Long-run elasticity of TE to DAR	0.21	1.82	0.07

Note
Dependent variable technical efficiency change (TEC). No. obs. 225.

acceptable for a second-stage analysis: the adjusted R-square is 0.48 for the cooperatives. The level of technical efficiency for the south is not statistically different respect with those of the north-centre. This is not surprising in the light of the results from the first stage where there was not much difference between firms located in the two areas. I control for dynamic adjustment processes by testing the significance of lagged values of technical efficiency and debt-to-asset ratio up to the second order. The first- and second-order lagged values of the level of technical efficiency enter significantly in the estimates, indicating the existence of a rather complex dynamic adjustment process. For cooperatives, serial correlation is not significant. The yearly dummy variables are generally insignificant apart from the one related to 2000 and they have a negative sign. Finally, more interestingly from our standpoint, the natural log of the debt-to asset ratio of the previous year, log[DAR(-1)], influences positively the growth of technical efficiency for cooperatives. The short-term impact of DAR on technical efficiency change is modest (0.06) but the long-term impact of DAR on the level of technical efficiency, as measured by the long-run elasticity, is higher (0.21). This long-run elasticity is significant for cooperatives. A further remark on the significance of DAR is that apparently it does not stem from an inappropriate estimation procedure in the presence of endogeneity. Indeed, regressing DAR on DAR[-1] and lagged values of technical efficiency yields largely insignificant values for the coefficients on the technical efficiency terms[8] (Bhargava, 1991). The evidence then favours the characterization of DAR as a long-run forcing variable with respect to TE, implying that OLS is an appropriate estimator in the regressions from Tables 4.4 and 4.5. Finally, the analysis has been repeated after excluding the 10 per cent of firms, extreme respect to the number of workers: 5 per cent among the biggest and 5 per cent among the smallest. The results are reinforced by and not sensitive to the omission of these extreme firms.

4.4 Concluding remarks

In this chapter, I have tested two hypotheses: (1) increases in financial pressure are followed by increases in technical efficiency, and (2) increasing product market competition and financial pressure can act as complementary mechanisms to help producers' cooperatives to improve efficiency. In particular, there has been substantial interest in the second hypothesis as the empirical evidence in its favour for conventional firms is rather ambiguous and unclear. Indeed, while the theory suggests that they are complementary mechanisms to improve productivity, the empirical evidence gives the opposite result. Nickell *et al.* (1997) have found no evidence of a positive interaction between increasing product market competition and financial pressure in fostering productivity growth. Indeed, Aghion *et al.* (2003) results suggest that financial pressure and competition are neither complementary nor substitutes. This contradiction in the empirical evidence may simply be due to the fact the firms considered in these empirical analyses are too heterogeneous and there is no clear channel through which these two mechanisms can jointly affect the firms' performance. Therefore, unlike the previous papers in this literature, I have decided to focus on cooperatives for two main reasons: first, they have been subject to increasing product market competition (following the process of liberalization and globalization in the product markets) while at the same time being chronically financially constrained (Birgegaard and Genberg, 1994); second, their organizational structure is such that there is a direct link between a co-op's technical efficiency and the workers' financial remuneration. As in the previous chapter, the analysis has been conducted in two stages. First, I have analysed these issues from a theoretical standpoint. So I have considered a cooperative where potential inefficiencies arise from the lack of alignment of interests of the membership and the workers. Indeed, workers supply the co-op with effort in exchange for a salary that is assumed to be a portion of the co-op's generated profits. In this type of environment, workers may find it profitable to hold-up their effort and this creates the conditions for a cooperative to appear inefficient. If so, either increasing product market competition or increasing financial pressure can improve the cooperative's technical efficiency as workers anticipate that their bonus may decrease following the change in the external environment and therefore they will be willing to increase their effort and so help to reduce inefficiency. However, when a cooperative is subject to both increasing financial pressure and product market competition, the net impact on technical efficiency may also be positive as long as the marginal productivity of effort is larger than 1. Empirically my analysis has been conducted on a panel of cooperative firms from Italy specializing in the production of wine over the period 1996–2001. The empirical results show that cooperative firms experience positive technical efficiency change following an increase in financial pressure. In addition, this relationship does hold for increasing product market competition as well. These results give support to the original hypothesis that increasing competition and financial pressure are complementary.

One limitation of this study is that I only consider a specific type of cooperative firm (producers' co-ops) in one sector (the wine sector). Therefore, further research is needed to test whether financial pressure and increasing product market competition are still complementary in other sectors and for other types of co-ops. Also additional work is required to identify exactly the channels through which these two mechanisms may have a different impact on co-ops' efficiency in different types of co-ops. Indeed, it is plausible to assume that these may be quite different for each type of cooperative: for the producers' cooperatives, it is obvious there is a direct link between competition, financial pressure and workers' effort; however, for workers' co-ops there must be obviously a different channel that links product market competition, financial pressure and co-ops' technical efficiency.

What are the policy implications of this study? It seems that co-ops are well equipped to cope with either increasing product market competition or increasing financial pressure; more correctly, their institutional structure allows them to have some "in-built" mechanisms that give them some slack that can be used to deal successfully with increasing external pressure. Like any other type of firm, co-ops can devise strategies that can help them to compete successfully in what have now become global product markets and one of these is to reduce the internal inefficiency where it is possible. However, when it is combined with increasing financial pressure, the effects on cooperatives' performance may even be reinforced and may eventually have a positive impact on the cooperatives' chances of survival. This obviously suggests that policy measures should be required to shelter financial constrained co-ops from the impact of increasing product market competition.

5 Self-employment and gender

How important are financial constraints?

5.1 Introduction

As mentioned in Chapter 2, the prevalence of women-owned businesses varies significantly across countries (Minniti *et al.*, 2004). In the USA nearly half of all privately owned firms (48 per cent) were women-owned in 2004 (Center for Women's Business Research, 2005). In Canada women constitute one-third of the total number of self-employed Canadians (CIBC, 2005). The prevalence of women-owned businesses in Finland is comparable to that of Canada. In Finland, 33 per cent of those 304,000 persons who were classified as self-employed in the 2003 Labour Force Survey were women (Arenius and Autio, 2006). Also, based on the data generated from the GEM (Global Entrepreneurship Monitor) database in 2002, the UK was found to rank 23rd out of 37 countries in terms of the ratio of female-to male-owned businesses. In 2003, with respect to the gap in the rate of venture creation by men and women, the UK ranked 7th out of 14 participating G7 and EU countries (Harding *et al.*, 2004). However high the growth rates are, the level of female entrepreneurship is still low. These low levels of involvement of women and individuals from a minority background into entrepreneurship in the UK is behind the perception at government level that there are still substantial segments of the population that could benefit from being self-employed but that still do not take advantage of this option because of the substantial entry barriers, mostly of a financial nature. In England a wide consultation exercise by the Small Business Support (SBS) unit (2003a) led to the launch of a "Strategic Framework for Women's Enterprise" (SBS, 2003b), in collaboration with the devolved administrations, various government departments, and with Prowess, a national UK network to promote women's enterprise. The strategic framework has identified six barriers to women's greater participation in entrepreneurial activity (SBS, 2003b, page 8): lack of appropriate business support; lack of access to finance; the impact of caring and domestic responsibilities; difficulties experienced in the transition from benefits to self-employment; lack of appropriate role models; and low levels of confidence and self-esteem.

However, the previous research in this area (as summarized in Chapter 2) has emphasized the complexity of the issues related to the finance of women-led companies and particularly the difficulty of trying to isolate and characterize any specific gender effect. Is it the case, for example, that lending institutions discriminate either deliberately or unwittingly against female entrepreneurs? Or, are female entrepreneurs simply more reluctant to seek external finance for their companies? Other factors linked to background, experience or even sector to which the company belongs may also be important in shaping males' and females' access to finance. So who is right and who is wrong? Are women financially discriminated against or do women self-select themselves and simply do not apply for external funding? These two opposite views are based on two different assumptions on how access to external funding first and then the self-employment choice are influenced by both gender and ethnicity. In the first case, it is assumed that financial institutions ration credit based on either gender or ethnic background, variables that are thought by external funders (in a presumably rather unconscious way) to be able to proxy for the capability the individual has of running a company successfully: in this case, the probability that individuals have of experiencing financial constraints is influenced directly by both the gender and its ethnic background; then only those that are not financially constrained can choose to become entrepreneurs. In the second view, the relationship between gender, ethnicity and financial constraints is much subtler than predicted by the first view: indeed, in this case it is possible that both women and individuals from a disadvantaged ethnic background expect to meet substantial future financial constraints when trying to have access to external funding to set up their own entrepreneurial activity. In other words, they may expect to be both credit rationed and to have unfavourable credit conditions. This may not necessarily mean they will be financially constrained once they apply for external funding; it simply means that based on the observation of the aggregate variables (in this case the small proportion of women and individuals from minority backgrounds having access to external credit) they expect to be credit-rationed based, indeed, on both their gender and ethnic background. This is possible because female applicants expect the terms of the loan agreement to be in favour of the financial institutions and therefore they are aware that most of the generated surplus will be appropriated (entirely or mostly) by the lender. So women prefer not to apply for external funding and therefore what is observed in the aggregate is the small proportion of loans granted to female applicants.

So a self-selection mechanism is at work where the probability an applicant has of approaching external funders is affected by both its gender and its ethnic background. This way, the self-employment choice is conditioned by either/both gender or/and ethnic background through the probability of approaching external funders. This last mechanism is consistent with the notion that economic agents may decide not to participate in a financial relationship if they expect that most of the surplus generated by them will be appropriated by the financial institution. In other words, economic agents internalize the impact of future financial constraints and this way, finance constraints affect the observed economic outcomes. Obviously it is possible that in reality a mix of the two mechanisms (namely, women do not get external funding and women do not seek external finance) can be at work and may contribute to explain the pattern that is observed in the data.

However, understanding which view prevails in reality is quite important as the policy interventions required for the two cases differ substantially. While in the first case, policy must be focused on removing the barriers to credit access, in the second case, policy-makers have to make sure that the perception of how financial intermediaries work among potential applicants changes among the potential applicants.

The purpose of this chapter is to analyse the relationship between financial constraints, gender, ethnic background and the individual's self-employment choice[1] using English data drawn from the *Household Survey of Entrepreneurship*, 2003 (the survey, henceforth) recently made available by the Small Business Support (SBS) Unit at the Department of Trade and Industry (DTI). The real advantage of this data-set is that it allows for information on the individuals' intentions to become self-employed in England and therefore it allows for assessing the importance of the perceived financial constraints on the future self-employment choice (or lack of). Empirically, I will use a variety of econometric methods to address the issues outlined above: I will first evaluate the extent to which financial constraints have an adverse impact on the probability of being self-employed and then whether these are compounded by gender and ethnic background. Therefore, I will first estimate a probit model where the self-employment choice appears as the dependent variable; measures of financial constraints, gender and ethnicity (and their interactions with the finance constraints) appear among the regressors. One problem with this specification is the potential endogeneity of the financial constraints measures. Therefore I will try to address this problem by using self-selection models to solve this potential problem. So in the second model, I will try to quantify the extent to which our two main variables of interest (gender and ethnicity) have an impact only on the probability individuals have of experiencing financial constraints first, so that only those who do not experience financial constraints can then become self-employed. This is equivalent to estimate a two-stage Heckman model where in the first stage I model the probability of experiencing financial constraints as a function of both gender and ethnic background, while in the second stage, I model the self-employment choice of those who have survived the first stage as a function of variables like the ability, human capital and so on. Finally, I will test whether gender and ethnicity affect mainly the access to external finance, while the self-employment choice is influenced by other factors (like previous experience as self-employed, current employment status and so on) that are independent of both gender and ethnicity. Again this will involve the estimation of a two-stage Heckman model where in the first stage the probability of accessing external funding is affected by both gender and ethnicity, while in the second stage I model the probability of self-employment for the individuals that have approached external funders as a function of their previous experience, education and so on.

The rest of the chapter is organized as follows. Section 5.2 illustrates the structure of the empirical analysis. More specifically, Section 5.2.1 provides a theoretical framework that looks at how financial constraints, gender, ethnic background and self-employment choice are related to each other. The format of the empirical analysis is also explained in detail in Section 5.2.2. Section 5.3 illustrates the data-set and provides a descriptive analysis of the main variables that will be used in the econometric analysis. Finally, Section 5.4 reports the main results, while Section 5.5 draws the main conclusions and gives an indication of potential caveats to the empirical analysis.

5.2 The model

5.2.1 The theoretical framework

As mentioned in the Introduction, the purpose of this chapter is to quantify the extent to which gender and ethnic background condition the self-employment choice through the lack of access to external finance (or financial constraints). Before this, it is necessary though to clarify the theoretical framework that underpins the empirical analysis. In the literature (surveyed in Chapter 2), the impact of the availability of external financial funding on the self-employment choice has been investigated by using the discrete models of career choice. In these models, an individual will choose to become self-employed if the utility from self-employment is greater than the one he gets from working for a company (Evans and Jovanovic, 1989). Therefore, most models of self-employment start by comparing the salaried income with the income an individual would earn from being self-employed. In this framework, this implies that an individual will become self-employed as long as:

$$w - y^{se} > 0,$$

where w is the wage income (obviously affected by a host of factors that may be beyond the control of the worker, like the state of industrial relations and so on) and y^{se} is the entrepreneurial income. However, the entrepreneurial income is affected by the ability an individual has to set up and run successfully a new company. I define this factor as "entrepreneurial ability" and I assume that it cannot be observed. Each individual in the population differs according to their "entrepreneurial ability" and I assume that the "entrepreneurial ability" is randomly distributed across all the segments of the population, or, in other words, it is independent of both the gender and the ethnic background of the single individual. Entrepreneurial ability is obviously important in determining whether or not the individual becomes an entrepreneur (self-employment choice). Indeed, I assume that entrepreneurial income is positively affected by the individuals' entrepreneurial ability. Therefore, entrepreneurial income can now be defined as:

$$y^{se} = R$$
$$R = R(\theta, e, K)$$

where R is a total revenue function which is affected positively by the individual's "entrepreneurial ability" (θ) or the capability of identifying and running a successful entrepreneurial project, by the entrepreneurial effort (e) and by the amount of financial capital available to the individual (K). The higher the ability, the larger the expected income, all else being equal; in the aggregate a large number of self-employed individuals will then be observed. However, the individual has to consider also the costs incurred when making the self-employment choice. There are three types of costs: (a) the foregone wage income: the higher the current wage income, the less likely the individual is to become an entrepreneur. Current wage income is influenced by the level of education, so that an increase in education reduces self-employment though it may improve the performance of those who do choose self-employment; (b) the costs of gathering funds to finance the project; and (c) the disutility cost of running a project that may be captured by a negative attitude towards self-employment. It is well documented that non-pecuniary lifestyle preferences (like the desire to be one's own boss or the desire to pursue not-for-profit objectives) play a significant role in influencing the self-employment decision (Blanchflower and Oswald, 1998).

Let me focus on (b). Under this heading, I group all the costs an individual has to bear to access external finance, among which the costs of persuading the external funders about the viability of the entrepreneurial project. Evans and Jovanovic (1989) argue that a liquidity constraint may occur when there is asymmetric information in the credit market, in the spirit of Stiglitz and Weiss (1981). In this case, entrepreneurs (borrowers) are more informed about both the profitability of the project and their own entrepreneurial ability than lenders, giving rise to problems of moral hazard and adverse selection. Indeed, external funders cannot observe the individual entrepreneurial ability and may attach to the project a different probability of success; therefore they will prefer to ration external funds on the basis of external indicators (gender, ethnic background and area of residence of the applicant), all assumed to be affecting the probability of entrepreneurial success. This implies that individuals applying for external funds either will receive less financial resources than they ask for or will not receive any financial support at all. However, consider the case where the potential borrower cannot observe completely his entrepreneurial ability or the profitability of his project (probably because it is his first entrepreneurial project). In this instance, the individual will try to infer the probability of being rationed by looking at aggregate data on the number of individuals that can successfully gather the financial capital for their project. If the proportion of credit-rationed women and individuals of minority background is high, then the potential borrower will anticipate that (s)he will be financially rationed; so (s)he will decide to self-select himself and therefore will not seek external funding.

These considerations suggest three potential models that relate the self-employment choice to both gender and financial constraints. Notice that rather than working with a highly structured model, I estimate reduced-form equations based on a linearization of the assumed probability function. In the first model I will test whether the individual's probability of becoming self-employed is affected by both (a) gender/ethnic background and (b) by the interaction terms between finance constraints and gender/ethnicity variables. In other words, the estimation of this model will help to quantify the extent to which finance constraints are compounded by both the gender and the ethnicity of the respondents. The empirical specification for this model is quite simple: the dependent variable is a dummy variable (DEP2ST) taking the value of 1 if the respondent is self-employed and 0 otherwise. Among the regressors I include the gender (sex) and/or the ethnic background of the respondent (White/Black/Asian) and an interaction term between the indicator of finance constraints – here proxied by a dummy variable (Finance Constraints) taking the value 1 if the respondent has experienced finance constraints – and the gender/ethnicity variables. I also control for the respondent's foregone wage income (proxied by either a variable that indicates whether the respondent has a degree[2] or his/her employment status), attitudes towards entrepreneurship, location and previous experience. I assume that ceteris paribus the probability of an individual becoming self-employed is affected positively by a subjective positive attitude towards entrepreneurship; equally the past experience of self-employment will enhance the individual's probability of becoming self-employed. Econometrically, this model will be estimated as a probit model. In formal terms, the equation that considers only the gender is the following:

$$DEP2ST_i = \alpha + \beta_1 Sex_i + \beta_2 FinCon_i + \beta_3 Sex_i * FinCon_i + \beta_4 x_i + u_i,$$

where x_i is the set of control variables. The specifications that focus on the ethnic background are the same with the only difference that instead of gender I control for the ethnic background (White/Black/Asian). One problem with this type of specification is that the probability of experiencing financial constraints may be endogenous and therefore I need to model its determinants. Therefore, the second model I will estimate allows us to test whether the individual's probability of going for self-employment is jointly conditioned by the respondent's gender and by the applicant's probability of experiencing finance constraints (that in turn is affected by an additional set of variables like the availability of collateral, education, location and so on). In other words I want to test the extent to which the probability of being financially constrained affects the individual's self-employment choice. Econometrically, this is equivalent to controlling for the fact that the probability of experiencing financial constraints is not random but may be dependent on specific factors like the individual characteristics of the applicants (gender, ethnic background and so on) and the availability of one's own private resources. I will therefore estimate a two-stage Heckman model: in the first stage the respondent's probability of experiencing finance constraints (Finance Constraints) is affected simultaneously by gender (Sex), ethnic background (White/Black/Asian), location (here measured by the region of residence – Region), education (Degree) and the collateral (Collateral) availability (here proxied by a dummy variable that controls for whether or not the applicant owns a house); in the second stage the probability of becoming self-employed is modelled as a function of gender, the respondent's foregone wage income (proxied by a variable indicating whether the respondent has a degree),[3] attitudes towards entrepreneurship, location and previous experience. In formal terms:

$$FinCon_i = \alpha' + \beta_1'Sex_i + \beta_2'White/Black/Asian_i + \beta_3'Sex_i*White/Black/Asian_i$$
$$+ \beta_3'\text{Re}gion_i + \beta_4'Degree + \beta_5'Landlord + \varepsilon_i$$

$$DEP2ST_i = \alpha + \beta_1 Degree_i + \beta_2 AttitudetowardsEntreprenuership_i$$
$$+ \beta_3 \text{Re}gion_i + \beta_4 \text{Pr}eviousExperience_i + u_i,$$

where $DEP2ST_i = 1$ if $FinCon = 0$.

Finally, in the third model, I will test whether a self-selection mechanism is at work in our data so that individuals from either a specific ethnic background or gender may decide not to apply for external funds; also I will estimate the impact that this decision has on the self-employment choice. Again, this model will be estimated by using the Heckman two-stage procedure (see Appendix B for more details on the Heckman estimation procedure) where two equations are estimated: the first equation models the self-selection mechanism where I try to identify the factors that affect the individual's choice of going for external finance; so I will model the probability of asking for external funds (DEP1ST) as a function of gender, education and location. The second equation models the self-employment choice and it is estimated only on the sample that "survives" the self-selection mechanism identified in the first equation. In this equation, I will model the probability of becoming self-employed as a function (among the others) of the previous experience (proxing for the entrepreneurial ability), the employment status (Employment Status) (measuring indirectly the foregone wage income) and the attitudes towards self-employment (as a measure of the disutility cost attached to running an entrepreneurial project). In formal terms:

$$DEP1ST_i = \alpha' + \beta_1'Sex_i + \beta_2'White/Black/Asian + \beta_3'Sex_i*White/Black/$$
$$Asian + \beta_4'Degree_i + \beta_5'\text{Re}gion_i + \varepsilon_i$$

$$DEP2ST_i = \alpha + \beta_1 EmploymentStatus_i + \beta_2 Attitu \det owards.$$
$$Entrepreneurship_i + \beta_3 EmploymentStatus_i + u_i,$$

where $DEP2ST_i = 1$ if $DEP1ST = 1$.

5.3 The Household Survey of Entrepreneurship (HSE), 2003

The bi-annual Household Survey of Entrepreneurship or HSE (SBS 2004)[4] was first introduced primarily to enable the Small Business Support Unit to gather information on the number of people *considering* going into business. It is nonetheless a useful source of data on start-ups and more importantly on the individuals' intentions to become self-employed in England. It surveys 10,002 individuals and segments them into *Thinkers* ("those who are thinking about becoming entrepreneurs", 11 per cent), *Doers* ("those who are already entre-preneurs through running their own business or by being self-employed", 13 per cent) and *Avoiders* ("those who are neither currently engaged in entrepreneurial activity nor thinking about doing so", 76 per cent). Each segment of the sample is asked different types of questions on the degree of access to external finance and whether they have encountered financial constraints. These questions are:

- **Thinkers:**
    - "And have you tried to obtain any finance for this new business in the past 12 months?" (Q13) and
    - "And did you have any difficulties in obtaining this finance from the first source you approached?" (Q16)
- **Doers:**
    - "In the past year have you tried to obtain finance for your business?" (Q40)
    - "Did you have any difficulties in obtaining this finance?" (Q44)
- **Avoiders:**
    - "And which two would you say are the biggest barriers to you starting a business or becoming self-employed?" (Q50).

The answers to these questions give an immediate indication of the access to external finance, the degree of financial constraints every segment of the popu-lation experiences, along with the impact this may have on the self-employment choice. In the 2003 Survey (the release I am using for this analysis), the propor-tion of Doers has fallen from 18 per cent and Avoiders increased from 70 per cent since the previous survey in 2001. It is not surprising to find in the survey, for example, that Doers are more highly represented amongst males, older people, minority background individuals (i.e. Asians, rather than Black people),[5] the edu-cated, higher social classes, those in rural areas and the South East. HSE indicates that 35 per cent of "avoiders" reported being prevented from starting a business by not being able to access finance for the business; whilst 27 per cent indicated that they would "not feel confident speaking to a bank manager about getting a business loan". There is not much variation by gender, but it is more likely for those who live in the 15 per cent most deprived wards (35 v. 26 per cent) and for Black and Caribbean/African and South Asian respondents (36 and 34 per cent v. 26 per cent). Similarly, there is evidence about fear of debt with 74 per cent overall, and with 80 per cent of women and 64 per cent of men and 76 per cent from the 15 per cent most deprived wards but with no breakdown by ethnic group. The analysis of barriers to starting a business also restates the points about

Table 5.1 Access to external funding: distribution of Thinkers by sex and ethnic origin

		White Yes	Black Yes	Asian Yes
Did try to obtain external finance	Male	32	3	
	Female	11	2	2
Did not try to obtain external finance	Male	401	32	28
	Female	283	17	17

Table 5.2 Difficulty to get access to external finance: distribution of Thinkers by sex and ethnic origin

		White Yes	Black Yes	Asian Yes
Male	Missing values	406	32	28
	Did experience FC	11	2	
	Did not experience FC	16	1	
Female	Missing values	284	19	17
	Did experience FC	5		
	Did not experience FC	6		2

Note
FC = Finance constraints.

Black and Asian respondents having difficulties accessing finance. Sources of finance are also analysed although differences by gender/ethnicity/location are not fully fleshed out.

The Data Annex provides some examples of the questions asked by the survey and also includes a number of indicative descriptive statistics for both Thinkers and Doers. Consistently with our a priori expectations, the proportion of Thinkers trying to get access to external finance is quite small and among these, the number of women from ethnic minorities is quite negligible (Table 5.1).

More than suggesting a potential problem of discrimination against women by ethnic minorities, this finding seems to confirm the common perception (as reported in the survey on this literature) that potential entrepreneurs may consider getting access to external finance quite difficult and therefore prefer to rely on more informal sources of funding (say friends and family circles) to set up their business. Table 5.2 shows the number of Thinkers who have experienced finance constraints, sorted by gender and ethnic origin.

White men do not have any difficulty to get access to external finance. Altogether a small number of women seem to have access to external funds even if in proportion they do not seem to be more financially constrained than men. Asian and Black women do not appear at all in the survey, suggesting the existence of a self-selection process prior to the application to external finance. Bank loans appear to be the favourite source of external funding for white Thinkers (both males and females) (Table 5.3).

Table 5.3 Primary source of external funding of Thinkers by sex and ethnic origin

		White	Black	Asian
Male	Equity investment	3		
	Bank overdraft	2	1	
	Bank loan	34		5
	Mortgage for property purchase or improvement	4	1	
	Loan from family/business partner/directors	2	4	
	Loan from a Community Development Finance Institution	2		
	Grant	11	1	3
	Other	18	2	
Female	Equity investment	3		
	Bank overdraft	1		
	Bank loan	18		4
	Mortgage for property purchase or improvement	5		
	Loan from family/business partner/directors	6		3
	Loan from a Community Development Finance Institution	1	1	
	Grant	5	1	
	Other	15		2

Table 5.4 Access to external finance: distribution of Doers by sex and ethic origin

		White	Black	Asian
Male	Did try to get external finance once	85	1	2
	Did try to get external finance more than once	39		1
	No	633	8	23
Female	Did try to get external finance once	41	2	1
	Did try to get external finance more than once	15		
	No	351	5	7

The residual category "OTHER" may seem to be an important source of external funding for Thinkers and probably some further analysis may be required to understand what type of funding source it picks up. Asian Thinkers prefer bank loans while Black women are virtually absent in this sub-sample.

I move now to the Doers.

Table 5.4 reveals quite strikingly that Doers are mostly of White origin while Black and Asian communities are clearly not represented in this sub-sample. Interestingly, finance constraints are mostly experienced by males of White ethnic background (Table 5.5). This does not mean that these are discriminated in their access to finance; it may simply hint to the fact that financial requests by men may be considered excessive by external funders and therefore these are not

Table 5.5 Distribution of doers by their difficulty to get finance, sex and ethnic origin

			White	*Black*	*Asian*
Male	Did you have any difficulties In obtaining this finance?	Yes, was unable to obtain any finance	12		1
		Yes, obtained some but not all of the finance required	7		
		Yes, obtained all the finance required but with some problem	11		
		No, had no difficulties in obtaining finance	93	1	2
Female	Did you have any difficulties in obtaining this finance?	Yes, was unable to obtain any finance	7		
		Yes, obtained some but not all of the finance required	1		
		Yes, obtained all the finance required but with some problem	1		
		No, had no difficulties in obtaining finance	46	2	1

always accommodated. Women do not have problems in having access to external funding. Indeed, women who have already started their business and have shown some entrepreneurial capability do not have more difficulties than men in getting financial resources. So, it seems that women encounter financial constraints mostly when they try to set up their business as at that stage they have not yet proven their worth. Finally, Black and Asian communities are totally absent in this sub-sample.

Tables 5.6–5.7 summarize the key characteristics of our sample (divided into Thinkers and Doers) by gender and ethnic background.

In terms of gender:

•   Overall, male Thinkers appear to be more qualified than female Thinkers. For both sexes, the most common qualifications are either a degree or GCSE. This is also true for Doers. However, among the male Doers there is a large proportion that does not hold a formal qualification.
•   A large proportion of Thinkers belongs to the 25–44 age bracket; also this distribution does not appear to differ substantially across gender. Doers appear to be concentrated in the 25–64 age bracket and it does not appear there is any difference according to the gender.
•   As for the employment status, a large proportion of male Thinkers appear to be currently in employment while female Thinkers are not. As for the Doers, the picture is more ambiguous: both male and female Doers

Table 5.6 Thinkers' characteristics by gender and ethnic background

	Sex		White	Black	Asian
	Male *(%)*	*Female* *(%)*	*(%)*	*(%)*	*(%)*
Education					
Degree	1.75	1.34	2.48	0.23	0.20
A-level	0.83	0.64	1.25	0.11	0.08
GCSE	1.07	0.78	1.64	0.09	0.09
Other	0.60	0.25	0.79	0.03	0.01
None	0.88	0.46	1.12	0.08	0.09
Age					
16–18	0.26	0.16	0.33	0.03	0.05
19–24	0.61	0.30	0.73	0.05	0.07
25–34	1.44	1.10	2.12	0.20	0.16
35–44	1.42	1.09	2.02	0.22	0.15
45–54	0.89	0.57	1.36	0.04	0.04
55–64	0.51	0.25	0.72	0.00	0.00
Current employment status					
Not employed	1.76	2.00	3.12	0.26	0.24
Employed	3.37	1.43	4.12	0.28	0.23
Previous experience					
Yes	3.26	2.48	4.83	0.43	0.27
No	1.87	0.99	2.45	0.11	0.20
Attitude towards entrepreneurship					
Negative/Neutral	1.49	0.82	2.05	0.05	0.10
Positive	3.64	2.65	5.23	0.49	0.37
Location					
North East	0.95	0.63	1.50	0.02	0.03
Yorks and Humber	0.22	0.20	0.39	0.00	0.02
East Midlands	0.33	0.15	0.45	0.02	0.01
East	0.15	0.10	0.22	0.01	0.02
London	0.72	0.45	0.66	0.29	0.09
South East	0.74	0.61	1.17	0.04	0.09
South West	0.41	0.21	0.61	0.01	0.00
West Midlands	0.33	0.26	0.45	0.04	0.07
North West	1.28	0.86	1.83	0.11	0.14
15 per cent most deprived wards	1.02	0.48	1.11	0.14	0.15
Others	2.60	1.90	4.01	0.16	0.25

appear to be mostly unemployed. This suggests a problem with the coding of the variable as these Doers are not unemployed but they are self-employed.

• Both male and female Thinkers appear to have some previous experience with self-employment. The proportion of male Doers with some previous experience in self-employment is higher than for female Doers; however,

Table 5.7 Doers' characteristics by gender and ethnic background

	Sex		White	Black	Asian
	Male (%)	Female (%)	(%)	(%)	(%)
Education					
Degree	2.61	1.55	3.74	0.10	0.17
A-level	0.96	0.62	1.50	0.02	0.03
GCSE	1.43	0.96	2.25	0.03	0.07
Other	1.11	0.55	1.53	0.00	0.02
None	2.11	0.66	2.65	0.01	0.06
Age					
16–18	0.09	0.02	0.09	0.00	0.02
19–24	0.24	0.11	0.29	0.03	0.02
25–34	1.25	0.58	1.62	0.01	0.16
35–44	2.39	1.39	3.49	0.04	0.10
45–54	2.21	1.27	3.32	0.05	0.04
55–64	2.04	0.97	2.86	0.03	0.01
Current employment status					
Not employed	6.61	3.74	9.62	0.14	0.29
Employed	1.61	0.60	2.05	0.02	0.06
Previous experience					
Yes	3.72	2.21	5.51	0.11	0.17
No	4.50	2.13	6.16	0.05	0.18
Attitude towards entrepreneurship					
Negative/Neutral	1.94	1.20	3.01	0.01	0.03
Positive	6.28	3.14	8.66	0.15	0.32
Location					
North East	1.43	0.82	2.14	0.00	0.03
Yorks and Humber	0.42	0.16	0.55	0.00	0.03
East Midlands	0.46	0.20	0.62	0.00	0.04
East	0.32	0.20	0.48	0.01	0.01
London	0.86	0.44	1.06	0.07	0.10
South East	1.33	0.69	1.85	0.05	0.04
South West	0.72	0.36	1.05	0.00	0.00
West Midlands	0.45	0.26	0.67	0.01	0.02
North West	2.23	1.21	3.25	0.02	0.08
15 per cent most deprived wards	1.12	0.37	1.29	0.02	0.11
Others	4.40	2.34	6.41	0.05	0.13

for both sexes, the proportion of Doers without any previous experience is quite high.

- The proportion of Thinkers (belonging to both sexes) with a positive attitude towards self-employment is large. The same applies to the Doers with the fraction of male Doers being quite substantial.
- Thinkers appear to be mostly located in the Northern and Southern regions. The proportion of Thinkers located in the Midlands is small. However, for

all the three areas, we can see that the fraction of male Thinkers is usually larger than that of female Thinkers. The same pattern applies to the Doers. Most Doers (male and female) are located in the North and the South of the country. Also, the proportion of male Doers is quite large.

So, in the sample, female respondents are less qualified than men; they may think about self-employment as an alternative to unemployment; they have a positive attitude towards self-employment; they are relatively young; they may have some previous experience (even if this is not true for the Doers); they are mostly located in the Northern and the Southern regions.

In terms of ethnic background, consistently with what presented before, I have sorted the respondents into three ethnic groups: White, Black and Asian. Generally speaking, the Black and Asian minorities appear to be under-represented in our sample. With this caveat in mind, these are the main characteristics of our respondents:

- White Thinkers are generally more qualified than those from other ethnic minorities. However, all respondents have some sort of qualification, with degrees and GCSE being the favourite ones. The same applies to the Doers, even if there is large proportion of White Doers who do not hold a qualification.
- Most White Thinkers belong to the 25–54 age bracket while most respondents from other ethnic backgrounds seem to be younger and belong to the 25–44 age bracket. White Doers are in the 35–64 age bracket, while the proportions of other minorities are quite small in all age brackets.
- As for the Thinkers, the three ethnic groups seem to be equally distributed among those who are employed and those who are not. In other words, there is not a clear pattern. Doers appear to be mostly unemployed and this applies to all three ethnic minorities.
- Most White Thinkers have a previous experience in self-employment along with the Black Thinkers. White and Asian Doers are almost equally split between those that have previous experience in self-employment and those who have not (with the proportion of White Doers without previous experience being larger than those with previous experience), while in the case of Black Doers, having some sort of previous experience matters.
- Finally, the proportion of Thinkers with a positive attitude towards self-employment is large and proportionally distributed across the three ethnic groups. The picture for the Doers is not different as a large proportion of Doers (from the three ethnic groups) has a positive attitude towards self-employment.
- In terms of location, most White Thinkers are located in the North and the South. A relatively large proportion of Black thinkers is located in the South, while Asian Thinkers are equally distributed between the North and the South. Doers share the same type of distribution: the North and the South are the areas of the country where most White and Asian Doers are located.

Finally, it is possible to notice that the proportion of respondents located in the 15 per cent most deprived ward is very small and it appears that most Thinkers and Doers are located elsewhere. The only exception is for respondents of a Black background as they appear to be equally distributed between the most deprived wards and the other ones.

5.4 The results

The empirical results for our three models are presented in Tables 5.8–5.11. A few comments about the results that are common to the three models are necessary here. First of all, I do not find evidence of any disadvantaged area effect (here proxied by the dummy variable for the 15 per cent most deprived wards) in any of the attempted specifications and therefore I have decided to drop this variable altogether. This is not surprising in the light of the descriptive analysis that showed that the proportion of respondents in the 15 per cent most deprived wards was rather negligible. Also, notice that the sample size for this model reduces substantially (230 observations) and this is due to the variable that measures the experienced finance constraints. Indeed, not all respondents decided to go for external finance and therefore the variable "finance constraints" does not apply to them.

The empirical results for the first model are presented in Table 5.8.

The results I get are quite interesting: gender and ethnic background do not enter significantly per se, but they influence the probability of being a Doer through the finance constraints variable. More specifically, the probability of a man becoming a Doer reduces to 49–50 per cent when finance constraints get tighter. More interestingly, women do not face these constraints. Having a previous experience in self-employment increases the probability of being a Doer by around 21–25 per cent. Equally, a switch to a negative attitude towards self-employment decreases the probability of being a Doer by 11 per cent. Also getting more mature improves the probability of becoming a Doer by 6.8–7 per cent; this last result indicates that becoming self-employed is a choice made at a later stage of the working career and it is not inconsistent with the results I find on the variable that measures the respondents' previous experience. The variables on the previous education and on the current employment status do not enter significantly and this shows that foregone income considerations do not matter.

The estimates for the second model are presented in Tables 5.9–5.10.

Generally speaking, either gender or ethnicity (and their interactions) does not have a significant impact on the probability of encountering financial constraints. This is not surprising given the fact that the proportion of respondents claiming to having been financially constrained is very small. Interestingly, the two significant variables in the first-stage equation are the regional variables (REGION) and the dummy variable on whether or not the respondent owns a house. This last result is definitely expected: financial constraints are exacerbated by the lack of collateral (which, however, can be perversely tied up to gender issues); as for

Table 5.8 Model 1: Probit estimates

Variables	Model 1		Model 2		Model 3		Model 4	
	Coefficient	T-ratio	Coefficient	T-ratio	Coefficient	T-ratio	Coefficient	T-ratio
Dependent variable: Probability of being a Doer								
Previous experience	0.252	3.760	0.234332	3.500	0.232	3.43	0.215	3.200
Attitude towards entrepreneurship	−0.113	−2.080	−0.11239	−2.030	−0.112	−1.95	−0.112	−1.940
Degree	0.053	0.960	–	–	0.057	1	–	–
Employment status	–	–	−0.21472	−1.020	–	–	−0.184	−0.900
Age	0.071	2.480	0.068581	2.360	0.079	2.74	0.079	2.700
Sex	0.106	1.910	0.106107	1.930	–	–	–	–
White	–	–	–	–	0.014	0.13	−0.00008	0.00000
Finance contraints*Sex	−0.492	−2.900	−0.52819	−3.310	–	–	–	–
Finance constraints*White	–	–	–	–	−0.248	−2.41	−0.242	−2.300

Note

$N = 230$. The observations are weighted by WEIGHT_1. We control for regions in all models.

Table 5.9 Model 2: Heckman two-stage model

	Model 1	
	Coefficient	*T-ratio*
Stage 2: Dep. Var. = DEP2ST		
Previous experience	1.93	1.99
Degree	0.49	0.71
Attitude towards entrepreneurship	−7.79	−5.29
Region	−0.18	−1.72
Sex	−0.25	−0.5
Stage 1: Dep. Var. = FC		
Region	0.09	2.41
Degree	0.17	0.72
Landlord	0.02	4.17
Sex	−1.13	−1.54
White	−0.91	−1.61
Sex*White	1.29	1.69
Correlation coefficient	−1.118	−1.52

Table 5.10 Model 2: Marginal effects

	Coefficient	*T-ratio*
Previous experience	0.011	1.32
Degree	0.003	0.66
Attitude towards entrepreneurship	−0.073	−1.53
Region	−0.001	−1.07
Sex	−0.002	−0.39

location, it is necessary to qualify these results: indeed, the regional variable picks up all those local factors (like underdevelopment, presence of criminality, low level of economic activity and so on) that can have an adverse impact on the likelihood of running a successful business and that therefore are taken into consideration by lenders in deciding whether or not to fund an entrepreneurial project. In the first stage, the probability of being a Doer is not affected significantly by gender, but rather by the previous experience and by the attitude towards entrepreneurship. However, marginal effects (Table 5.10) are generally not significant, showing that from this sample it is not possible to draw conclusions regarding the whole population.

The results for the third model are presented in Table 5.11 while the marginal effects are presented in Table 5.12.

Notice that again the marginal effects are only presented for the second-stage equation. Generally speaking, the probability of having access to external finance increases if the respondent is male and white. This implies that women of white ethnic background decide to self-select themselves and prefer not to seek external finance. For the subset of individuals that decide to go for external

Table 5.11 Model 3: Heckman two-stage model

	Model 1		Model 2		Model 3	
	Coefficient	T-ratio	Coefficient	T-ratio	Coefficient	T-ratio
Dependent variable: DEP2ST						
Previous experience	0.261	2.940	0.366	0.680	0.287	0.520
Degree	0.199	1.730	0.245	0.880	0.226	1.010
Attitude towards entrepreneurship	−0.174	−2.550	−0.213	−1.070	−0.138	−0.780
Employment status	−0.295	−2.040	−0.280	−1.040	−0.207	−0.780
Region	−0.006	−0.240	−0.021	−0.350	−0.014	−0.160
Constant	−1.632	−9.410	−1.609	−7.570	−1.649	−8.580
Dependent variable: DEP1ST						
Region	0.002	0.120	0.005	0.290	0.003	0.170
Degree	0.096	0.990	0.094	0.980	0.101	1.030
Sex	0.387	2.540	−0.118	−1.030	−0.073	−0.490
White	0.233	3.270	–	–	–	–
Asian	–	–	–	–	−0.397	−0.910
Black	–	–	−0.054	−0.260	–	–
Sex*White	−0.529	−3.170	–	–	–	–
Sex*Black	–	–	0.575	1.260	–	–
Sex*Asian	–	–	–	–	0.440	1.150
Constant	−1.460	−10.290	−1.264	−9.700	−1.244	−9.650
Correlation coefficient	3.803	2.200	2.266	0.850	2.844	0.490

Note
Initial number of observations: N = 2106. The observations are weighted by WEIGHT_1.

Table 5.12 Model 3: Marginal effects

	Model 1		Model 2		Model 3	
	Coefficient	T-ratio	Coefficient	T-ratio	Coefficient	T-ratio
Previous experience	0.041	2.720	0.064	0.490	0.046	0.420
Degree	0.033	1.620	0.045	0.580	0.038	0.700
Attitude towards entrepreneurship	−0.029	−2.310	−0.040	−0.670	−0.023	−0.570
Employment status	−0.047	−2.020	−0.049	−0.710	−0.033	−0.600
Region	−0.001	−0.240	−0.004	−0.290	−0.002	−0.150

finance, an improvement in the attitudes towards self-employment implies an increase of 2 per cent of the probability of becoming a Doer; also becoming unemployed means that the individual is less likely to become a Doer by 4 per cent. Finally, an increase of the previous experience is likely to increase the probability of becoming a Doer by 4 per cent. In these models, the regional and deprived area variables are not significant, showing that there is no location effect at work in either the self-selection mechanism or the self-employment choice. I have tried to run these same specifications on respondents of different ethnic background but I have not been able to find significant results. This suggests that in the case of Black and Asian minorities other factors are at work that cannot be captured adequately by this type of model.

Altogether these results confirm my initial hypothesis. In my population, women (from any ethnic background) do not appear to be financially constrained because of their gender but only because of the lack of collateral; also, in the population, the expectation of being financially constrained in the future deters women from seeking external finance for their investment projects. These results confirm my initial hypothesis, namely that gender and ethnic background condition the probability of seeking for external finance rather than the probability of being financially constrained. Of course, these results do not identify exactly why this is the case. Consistently with my view on how financial constraints affect economic outcomes, I can only conjecture that this is so because female applicants anticipate that most of the surplus generated by the entrepreneurial project will be appropriated back by the lender. Indeed, it would be interesting to devise an empirical strategy that allows to test whether this type of mechanism is at work in the population.

Some caveats to the empirical analysis are important and they mostly arise from the data I have used. Also, the employment status variable for the Doers does seem to have a problem as most Doers are classified as unemployed. Second, Black and Asian communities seem to be under-represented in the sample. This point may simply reflect the proportion in the population of individuals from both the Black and the Asian communities. To clarify this point, it would be helpful to have some information on the whole population and on the population of entrepreneurs. Third, this analysis of the survey is, because of the way the sample is constructed, more focused on "Thinkers" and "Doers", i.e. those who are either engaged in or thinking about undertaking some enterprise activity. I have not considered at all the individuals who claim not to be interested in becoming self-employed (the so-called Avoiders); this is mostly due to data availability as they are not asked the same type of questions on external finance and experienced financial constraints as the Doers and Thinkers do. However, it would be advisable to devise questions for the Avoiders that mirror those for the two other segments of the sample. Also, the data analysed here are purely cross-sectional, however, and while this makes it possible to draw some inferences about the effects of financial constraints on start-up rates, for example, it is impossible to draw implications on the unobserved heterogeneity among individuals that clearly affects whether applicants experience financial constraints and then their self-employment choice. In other words, financial constraints may also depend on the unobserved heterogeneity of the individuals in the sample and the use of cross-sectional data prevents from controlling for all these additional factors that may affect financial constraints. Also, cross-sectional data do not make it possible to control the impact of financial constraints on the subsequent success of the start-up companies. Similarly, it proved difficult from the existing survey data to draw any firm conclusion about the impact of finance shortages on subsequent business performance. Both require more longitudinal follow-up of individuals that have participated in cross-sectional surveys and this as a research priority. In each case, sample sizes were relatively small and inferences about either group were unlikely to be robust. The policy significance of each issue is likely to mean that developing appropriate sampling methodologies to identify ethnicity and spatial effects on financial barriers are also likely to be issues for the future. Finally, it is worth noting that in each of these general surveys the proportion of firms and individuals reporting that they were involved in entrepreneurship and that they had experienced difficulties in accessing finance is relatively small.

5.5 Concluding remarks

In this chapter I have estimated three different empirical models of career choice in an attempt to quantify the extent to which financial constraints affect negatively the involvement of women and individuals from a minority background into entrepreneurship. The analysis has been conducted on the Household Survey on Entrepreneurship, 2003, compiled by the SBS Unit and a valuable source on the intentions respondents have to become self-employed in England. In the first model I have estimated directly the impact of financial constraints on the self-employment choice to understand how these interact with gender and ethnic background to impact negatively the self-employment choice. Afterwards, I have tried to model the impact of gender and ethnic background on the probability of experiencing financial constraints in an attempt to model the potential sources of endogeneity that could affect the first model. Finally, in the third model I have assumed that gender and ethnic background affect the probability of seeking external funding as women may expect to be either credit rationed or to have less favourable credit conditions than men.

The key findings from our empirical analysis are the following: (a) being female or from an ethnic background does not appear to enhance the finance constraints that adversely impact the self-employment choice. On the contrary, these are compounded by the lack of collateral and by the location; (b) a self-selection mechanism is at work where women (from any ethnic background) anticipate encountering substantial financial constraints (even if this may not necessarily be justified) and then implicitly decide not to be self-employed. Interestingly enough, being located in a very deprived area does not affect the probability of becoming self-employed, unlike what the previous literature suggests according to which rates of female self-employment in the northern regions are up to half of those in the more economically dynamic south (Fielden and Dawe, 2004).

Taking these points together suggests that females in the general population perceive stronger financial barriers to business start-up than males, and this may discourage them from seeking external financial support for business start-ups. I find no evidence, however, that where females do seek finance for start-ups they are less likely to obtain it than males or that financial institutions condition their decision of awarding external finance to different variables than in the case of male applicants: indeed, collateral availability is the key decision variable. This is suggestive of a dominant demand rather than a supply side effect. In either case, however, the effect is similar – that gender differences in access to finance are reducing female start-up rates.

From a policy perspective the key points here are that female start-up rates are being reduced by (a) the general perception of stronger financial barriers to start-up among females, and (b) their unwillingness to seek external finance for business start-ups. Addressing these issues is likely to require a combination of measures designed both to redress the perception that it is more difficult for females to access business finance and to encourage potential female entrepreneurs to be more ambitious in seeking external finance. Successfully addressing these issues alone will not, however, fully close the gap between male and female start-up rates. Indeed, it is also important to redress the balance between lenders and borrowers in such a way that female applicants do not perceive that most of the surplus will be appropriated by the lenders afterwards.

Data annex

The data for the empirical analysis have been drawn from the *Household Survey on Entrepreneurship*, 2003 data file with sample observations being weighted to give results representative of the UK working-age population (variable: weight_1) (see Table 5.13).

List of variables

Dependent variables:

DEP2ST = this is a dummy variable taking the value of 1 if the respondent is a Doer and 0 otherwise. This variable has been constructed by combining the dummy variables indicating Thinkers and Doers in the data-set.
DEP1ST = this is a dummy variable taking the value of 1 if the respondent is trying to get access to external finance and 0 otherwise. This variable has been constructed by combining the answers to Q13 for the Thinkers and Q40 for the Doers.

Independent variables:

Degree: a dummy variable taking the value of 1 if the respondent has a degree or not.
Region: this enters in M1 as a group of dummies indicating the regions (with the South East being the omitted category). In M2, it enters as a continuous variable with the largest values indicating the Midlands and the Southern regions.

Table 5.13 Household survey of Entrepreneurship 2003 variables

Dependent variable	Important regressors	Variables of interest
Are you trying to start up a business?[1] **ma000001** (*mainact: All thinkers*) **2** (*mainact: Serious thinkers*), 3 (*mainact: Less serious thinkers*)	Access to finance: **diff_fin** i.e. *Difficulties obtaining finance* – Yes, did not obtain finance – Yes, obtained some but not all – Yes, obtained all with problems – No difficulties Also **q13** (*Q13 Tried to obtain any finance for this new business in the past 12 months?*) and **q16** (*Q16 Difficulties in obtaining finance from the first source?*)	Gender: **sex_bk** (*Male or Female recorded/coded*) and **sex**
	type of finance: **q1000032, 33 etc to q1000051** (*Q14 What type of finance did you seek?/Would you be most likely to seek?*) with full list Info on amount also (**q15:** *Q15 Approximately how much finance did you seek?*)	Ethnicity: **et000001 – 10** (*ethnic group*) and **q79** (*Q79 How would you describe your ethnic origin?*)
	source of finance: Above variables indicate whether from bank, CDFI etc	Location: **de000001** (*dep_index: Deprivation index*)
	access constraints: Again **q16** indicates whether able to obtain finance, or only part etc	Age: **age_bk** (*Age*)
	help/advice: Two specific variables/sets 1. Relating to effectiveness of advice: **q17** (*Q17 Financial organization/source offer you any help?*) and **q17a** (*Q17A Did you use this advice to submit an improved application?*) and **q17b** (*Q17B Did you eventually go on to obtain finance for your business?*) 2. Future likely sources of advice: **q2000001 – 33** (*Q20 Organizations or contacts would you be likely to use for business support or advice in the future?*) Big list	Education/skills: **edu** (*Highest level of Nationally recognized qualification*)
		industrial activity: **cu000001 – 10** (*current employment e.g. self-emp, ft, pt emp, unemp etc*)

Gender: this is a dummy variable set to 1 for men.

Age: this is a set of dummy variables taking the value of 1 for each respondent who is in a specific age bracket and 0 otherwise.

Employment status: this is a dummy variable taking the value of 1 if the respondent is NOT in either full- or part-time employment.

15 per cent most deprived wards: this is a dummy taking the value of 1 if the respondent is located in one of the most deprived areas and 0 otherwise.

Attitude towards entrepreneurship: this is a dummy variable taking the value of 0 if the respondent has a positive attitude towards entrepreneurship and 1 otherwise.

Finance constraints: this variable is a dummy variable taking the value of 1 if the respondent has experienced financial constraints and 0 otherwise. This variable has been constructed by combining the answers to Q16 (for the Thinkers) and Q44 (for the Doers).

Ethnic Background: this is a set of dummy variables taking the value of 1 if the respondent has a specific ethnic background (White, Black and Asian, respectively) and 0 otherwise.

Past Experience: this variable takes the value of 1 if the respondent has previous entrepreneurial experience and 0 otherwise.

Landlord: this is a dummy variable taking the value of 1 if the respondent does not own a house and 0 otherwise.

Appendix: sample selection models

The purpose of this appendix is to briefly introduce the logic and the econometrics behind the sample selection models used in Chapter 5. The basic intuition behind these models is quite simple. Consider a population where a certain outcome variable (in the models from Chapter 5 the self-employment choice) is not observed for all the individuals of the population. It is then possible to assume that this variable y is only observed if some criterion is met, for instance if the individual has been successful in applying for external funds (using again the example from Chapter 5). In turn, whether or not this criterion is met may depend on a set of additional exogenous variables. It has been proved that if the selection problem is not considered and the outcome equation is estimated by using OLS, the slope estimates are biased. Therefore, in order to avoid this problem and to get asymptotically efficient estimators, the Maximum Likelihood estimator can be used that estimates simultaneously the selection mechanism and the outcome equation.

Note

1 The variables covered in the table relate to those starting a business (i.e. '**Thinkers**'). There are other variables in the HSE for '**Doers**' (those who are already running a business), which correspond to these questions, i.e. **q40** (*Q40 In the past year have you tried to obtain finance for your business?*); **q4000001 – 15** (*Q42 What type of finance did you seek?*); **q43** (*Q43 And approximately how much finance did you seek?*); and **q44** (*Q44 Did you have any difficulties in obtaining this finance?*); and questions also on advice and whether that helped (i.e. **q45, q45a, q45b**). However, as expected, these questions are obviously not asked to '**Avoiders**' (those choosing not to start a business and who don't intend to).

So a typical sample selection model is made of two equations:

$$y_i^* = x_i' \beta + u_i$$
$$y_i = y_i^* \text{ if } z_i = 1$$
$$y_i \text{ not observed if } z_i = 0$$

$$z^* = w' \alpha + e_i$$
$$z_i = 0 \text{ if } z_i^* \leq 0$$
$$z_i = 1 \text{ if } z_i^* > 0,$$

where both e and u are independent errors with mean equal to zero and a constant variance. It is assumed that the two errors are correlated. The first equation is the selection equation while the second one is the outcome equation. In the first equation, a latent continuous variable (normally distributed) y* is a function of a set of regressors x. However, it is possible to observe y* if the variable z takes the value 1. z is the realization of a latent variable z* that is in turn affected by a set of variables w'. If z* is positive, then z will take the value of 1.

6 Conclusions

Time has arrived now to draw some conclusions from the analysis conducted so far. As mentioned in the Introduction to the book, the main purpose of this study was to identify and understand how financial constraints affect economic agents' behaviour (and so economic outcomes) by changing the incentive structure they are exposed to. This topic is quite interesting in itself because understanding how financial constraints affect the choices individuals make holds important academic and public policy ramifications, given the pervasiveness of finance constraints especially in countries where financial markets are not very well developed and therefore problems of asymmetric information are particularly strong and binding. Now, this research topic is not new in itself: indeed, it is true that there exists a substantial literature that has analysed the conditions under which financial constraints arise and the impact that they can have on economic outcomes. Indeed, the last 30 years have witnessed a dramatic revival of research on credit constraints and their origin. It is now established that credit constraints arise because of the asymmetric distribution of information among borrowers and lenders; it is also accepted that this affects the optimal properties of the competitive equilibrium in the credit market and firms' capital accumulation process. These advances have been made possible by the path-breaking developments in the economics of information and incentives after the Akerlof's seminal paper (1970) that has emphasized the potential inefficiencies in trade arising when either of the parties involved has an informational advantage. Thanks to a series of influential papers by Stiglitz and Weiss (1981) and Williamson (1986) the formal apparatus devised to analyse trade under imperfect information has been extended naturally to the study of the credit market. Both authors conclude that informational asymmetries create an incentive problem, inducing banks to ration credit. Indeed, in both adverse selection and moral hazard, an increase of the interest rate on loans may adversely affect the rate of return to banks, and therefore these may wish to hold the interest rate below the market clearing level since raising the rate would lower the bank's returns. Therefore some borrowers will be rationed in equilibrium and will not get enough financial resources to carry out their activities.

Afterwards, a complementary stream of literature (mostly empirical) has analysed the implications of these informational imperfections on economic agents. Most research has, though, focused on the direct impact of credit rationing on firms and consumers. So, one prediction from these models of credit rationing is that the cost of borrowing for some firms (typically small firms without a long track record) will be higher than in the case with perfect information. This implies that for these firms borrowing becomes too expensive and therefore they will prefer to cut their productive activities (for instance, investment expenditure), unless they can use their own financial resources (either as collateral or for direct funding of the investment). This way, credit rationing prevents potentially profitable and welfare-enhancing projects from being funded and allow borrowers' personal characteristics (that do not necessarily have any bearing on the future profitability of a project) to affect the characteristics of the market equilibrium. Therefore, the demand for investment (and for labour for that matter) of a firm that is credit rationed will depend positively on its balance sheet position as a strengthened balance sheet implies it has more available resources to either use directly to fund the investment project or as collateral to obtain outside funds. Another prediction from this theoretical literature is that financial institutions will not be willing to fund the formation of new companies unless the individual applicant is endowed with sufficient wealth that can then be used as collateral for the project. At a macroeconomic level, financial constraints can help to amplify negative productivity shocks as financially constrained firms will see their balance sheet position deteriorate very fast during a recession and this will increase even more the cost of external borrowing, reinforcing the negative impact of the initial productivity shock on the firm's level of production and demand for inputs.

Generally speaking, the economic literature that looks at the relationship between economic outcomes and financial constraints is characterized by a recurring theme: financial constraints are "bad" as, by changing the cost of external funding, they alter the incentives structure economic agents are exposed to in such a way that the resulting economic outcomes are inefficient. The theoretical perspective adopted in this book is different though. I still agree with the notion that the main impact of financial constraints is that of increasing the cost of borrowing; however, I argue that financial constraints may have additional effects (some of which can be desirable and some undesirable) that are always rooted in the fact that the incentives of the economic agents change due to the finance constraints. These additional effects, I claim, can also create the conditions for finance constraints to have a positive impact on the economic outcomes. I conjecture there are two main mechanisms that make this possible: first, I argue that financial constraints act as mechanisms that affect the ex-post distribution of rents among the many agents that have contributed to create them. So in this perspective, a tightening of the financial constraints (or even the expectation of an increase in financial pressure) changes (or is expected to change) the way the rents are distributed ex post and if the increase in financial constraints is deemed to be permanent, this will directly affect the behaviour of the economic agents that contribute to the generation of these rents. So, for instance, consider a firm that is financially constrained as it cannot have access to the full amount of financial resources it requires to fund its productive activities; the direct effect of these financial constraints is obviously the increase of the cost of capital and therefore a reduction in the investment expenditure. However, the impact of financial constraints may be felt more by managers than by the owners of the firm as the increasing financial pressure may reduce the managers' financial bonuses rather than the dividends to the owners. So one consequence generated by the additional financial pressure (beyond the increase of the external cost of borrowing) is that of inducing the managers to increase their effort as long as there exists a link between managers' effort and their financial bonuses. In this case, what happens is quite simple: the distribution of the rents generated by the firm is shifted in favour of the shareholders following an increase of the financial constraints and therefore managers have now the incentive to change their behaviour and contribute more to the firm's activity (by increasing their effort). Second, if some economic agents are financially constrained then this indicates that the contractual relationship between borrowers and lenders is in favour of the lenders so that most of the surplus generated by the borrowers will be appropriated by the lender through the repayments and interest rates. So, if an individual expects particularly unfavourable credit conditions, then he may decide not to apply for funding altogether and eventually give up a potentially profitable investment project. A typical example is the case of self-employment: consider an individual who on the basis of its personal characteristics (gender, personal background, residence in a poor area and so on) expects to be financially constrained (on the basis of some aggregate indicator, like average number of successful loan applicants from disadvantaged areas and so on). In this case, just the expectation of future financial constraints can induce this individual to give up setting up a new company and what is then observed in the aggregate is the low number of new firms led by individuals from disadvantaged areas, for instance, or with some specific personal characteristics, more generally.

If this general perspective is accepted, then interesting empirical findings can now be explained. Indeed, it has already been mentioned in the Introduction by the study of Nickell and Nicolitsas (1999) who find that firms experience an improvement in productivity following a tightening of financial constraints. One way to rationalize these findings is indeed by conjecturing that the tightening of the financial constraints is reducing the share of the firm's surplus managers are entitled to and therefore they prefer to cut the firm's inefficiencies so to increase the generated surplus and then their share. Also by using this theoretical perspective it is possible to reconcile the somehow contrasting findings of the literature on gender and new business formation. Indeed, while the theoretical literature suggests that the supply of new external funds may be conditioned by the gender of the applicant, the empirical literature could not find the definitive evidence that this is indeed the case. More likely, what is at work is what has been termed in the study a "demand effect" where women do not seek external funds (i.e. they do not demand funds) as they expect that most of the surplus generated by their investment project will be appropriated by the financial institutions.

To analyse these issues, I have focused on three cases in this book. In the first one (Chapter 3), I have analysed the relationship between financial constraints and technical efficiency in the attempt to identify the conditions under which firms' technical efficiency can improve following an increase of the financial pressure firms are exposed to. In the second case (Chapter 4), I have tried to ascertain the extent to which increasing financial pressure coupled with increasing product market competition can improve technical efficiency in producers' cooperatives. Finally, in the third case (Chapter 5), I have analysed the impact of financial constraints on the formation of new firms led by women. Let me consider the findings for each of the three cases separately.

Technical efficiency and financial constraints. In Chapter 3 I have analysed the impact of financial constraints on the evolution of technical efficiency over the period 1989–1994 for a sample of firms drawn from Italian manufacturing. The results are quite interesting and in some sense counterintuitive. Indeed, conventional wisdom assumes that firms whose financial conditions worsen over time will prefer to cut their investments and then reduce the level of production. So in this case, the impact on the firm's performance of increasing financial pressure should be either negative or in the best case negligible. However, I argue that this is first-best reasoning that forgets the fact that firms are exposed to more than one distortion and that therefore can act on one distortion (say, internal inefficiency) so as to reduce the impact of a second one (in our case, the increasing financial constraints). This is exactly the case I consider here. So in the theoretical model I focus on a firm that is characterized by the division between ownership and control (as it is typical in modern corporations). It is well known that in this case, managers are not the firm's residual claimants and therefore they can pursue their own objectives that may not necessarily be consistent with the objective of profit maximization. In my model, I assume managers contribute to the creation of the firm's surplus by providing effort. However, I also assume they prefer to maximize their own private benefits (say, private consumption) from the relationship with the firm rather than the overall surplus. This creates the conditions for the hold-up problem that generates the firm's technical inefficiency. How can an increase in financial pressure improve the firm's technical efficiency in this sort of environment? The key condition here is the existence of a link between the manager's financial remuneration (in other words, a component of its private benefit) and the firm's performance. In itself, this is not surprising; indeed, it is a central tenet of corporate governance research that performance-related payments have indeed the potential of re-aligning individual interests with those of the company. What is new here is how this interacts with the financial constraints. Indeed, consider an increase in the financial pressure the firm is exposed to. Managers anticipate that the potential worsening of the credit conditions can affect adversely their financial remuneration and therefore they will try to offset this by increasing their effort, so contributing to reduce the level of technical inefficiency. So, in this case, the financial constraints can work as the external mechanism that realigns the manager's incentives with those of the ownership by changing the surplus sharing once the production has taken place. Empirically, this model has a clear prediction: the tightening of financial constraints is followed by increases in firms' technical efficiency. I have tested empirically this prediction for a panel of Italian firms from 1989 to 1994, divided into eight sectors. Technical efficiency has been measured as the distance from a benchmark (so-called production frontier) that provides the best practice for the sector. The results tend to confirm our prediction: indeed financial constraints can play an important role in explaining improvements in technical efficiency. Indeed, firms may decide to offset the negative impact of increasing financial pressure by reducing the organizational slack. This does not imply that financial constraints are always good. Indeed, it is important to recall that they slow down innovation at firm's level, and so economic growth, and that therefore the overall impact of financial constraints on the performance of the economic system can be negative. This result is also important as it shows that increases in total factor productivity following increases in financial constraints (as shown in the previous studies) are due to the reduction of the organizational slack. This work can be easily extended into two directions. First, it may be of interest to analyse the impact of equity rationing on technical efficiency; to this purpose, the theoretical model presented in this chapter may be extended to account for equity rationing and can be used to derive the relationship between technical efficiency and equity rationing. Second, an interesting extension might be that of testing whether financial pressure maintains its role as a disciplining mechanism for managers when other disciplining mechanisms are available (like a majority shareholder or an external banker).

Financial pressure, product market competition and technical efficiency of producers' co-ops. In Chapter 4, the analysis has focused on the relationship among product market competition, financial pressure and technical efficiency. Indeed, in the theoretical perspective adopted in this book, financial pressure may align the interests of a group of agents in a firm with those of the ownership by changing the way the generated surplus is distributed among the several agents in the firm once production has taken place. So indirectly this disciplining effect of financial pressure is not very different from the impact on firms of increasing product market competition. Hence, the interest in the relationship between the two mechanisms that is at the basis of the study contained in Chapter 4. Indeed, if the two mechanisms are complementary, it would imply that firms with a higher debt-to-asset ratio (or more indebted firms) may be more sensitive to increasing product market competition with the result that there exists a potential non-linearity in the impact of competition policies on firms' performance (Aghion and Griffith, 2005). Of course, this potential relationship has already been noticed before, although there is not a clear conclusion on whether these two mechanisms do either complement or offset each other. Indeed, while the theory suggests that these are complementary to improve productivity, the empirical evidence gives the opposite result. Nickell *et al.* (1997) has found no evidence of a positive interaction between increasing product market competition and financial pressure in enhancing productivity growth. Also, the results by Aghion *et al.* (2003) suggest that financial pressure and competition are neither complementary nor substitute mechanisms to increase firm's innovation (and so productivity). This contradiction between theory and empirical evidence may simply be due to the fact the firms considered in these two analyses are too heterogeneous and therefore there is no clear link among firms' performance, individual behaviour and external environment. Therefore I focus my analysis on a more homogeneous sub-set of firms – producers' cooperatives – where the institutional structure identifies a clear relationship between the organization's performance and the workers' private benefit. Indeed, the argument behind this choice is quite simple: I suggest that both financial pressure and product market competition are complementary as long as there is a clear link between financial remuneration (or individual benefit) and firms' performance and indeed the advantage of using a data-set of cooperative firms is that institutionally there is a clear link between the two. Also, I have decided to focus on cooperatives as they have been subject to increasing product market competition (following the process of liberalization and globalization in the product markets) while being chronically financially constrained; therefore they are the perfect case-study for my analysis.

I have so tested two hypotheses: (1) increasing product market competition and financial pressure can act as either substitute or complementary mechanisms to help producers' cooperatives to improve technical efficiency, and (2) increasing financial pressure is followed by increasing technical efficiency. As in the previous chapter, the analysis has been conducted in two stages. First, I have considered these issues from a theoretical standpoint. So I have started from a cooperative where potential inefficiencies arise from the lack of alignment of interests of the membership and of the workers. In this type of environment, either increasing product market competition or increasing financial pressure can improve the cooperative's technical efficiency as workers anticipate that their bonus may decrease following the change in the external environment. This implies that they will be willing to increase their effort and this will help to reduce inefficiency. Also, when a cooperative is subject to both increasing financial pressure and product market competition, the net impact on technical efficiency is still positive as long as the marginal productivity of effort is larger than 1. In other words, there must be increasing returns in the effort so that the increasing effort can counterbalance the adverse impact of the jointly increasing financial pressure and product market competition. Empirically, the analysis has been conducted on a panel of cooperative firms from Italy specializing in the production of wine over the period 1996–2001. The empirical results show that the cooperative firms experience positive technical efficiency change following an increase in financial pressure. In addition, this relationship does hold when product market competition increases as well. These results give support to the original hypothesis that increasing competition and financial pressure are complementary as long as there is a clear relationship between individual remuneration and firm's performance. This result can be explained by recalling that, when external pressure increases, they will increase effort as they expect their wage to be affected adversely by the joint increase of product market competition and financial pressure. The study has two main limitations. First, I do not consider the possibility of strategic interactions among workers when deciding the level of effort to supply. This is a modelling choice that, however, does not affect the final result as it is possible to show that the interaction among workers may create the conditions for the increasing returns to scale condition that is necessary for the result. Second, I only consider a specific type of cooperative firms (producers' co-ops) in one sector (the wine sector). Therefore, further research is needed to test whether the results I get still hold in other types of co-ops. Also, additional work is required to identify exactly the channels through which these two mechanisms affect technical efficiency in different types of co-ops. Indeed, it is plausible to assume that these may be quite different for each type of cooperative: for the producers' cooperatives, it is obvious there is a direct link between competition, financial pressure and workers' effort; however, for workers' co-ops there must obviously be a different channel that connects product market competition, financial pressure and co-ops' technical efficiency.

These results are quite important under two respects. From a theoretical standpoint, they support the hypothesis (formalized in the theoretical model) that the two mechanisms are complementary as long as the workers' individual remuneration is directly affected by firms' performance. Also, these results are important for policy purposes. Indeed, it is well known that increasing globalization of product markets has put some pressure on co-ops that for structural reasons tend also to be financially constrained. Not surprisingly, there has been a call for direct policy interventions aimed at defending the co-ops from the impact of the increasing product market competition. However, our results show that the negative impact on co-ops of both increasing financial pressure and increasing product market competition has been overemphasized in the popular literature. Indeed, these two mechanisms can work together in this respect and that co-ops, like any other organization, can reduce their organizational slack when they are under pressure. This is indeed possible exactly because a cooperative's organizational structure is such that the co-ops' performance can affect directly the workers' remuneration. This implies that co-ops have some internal mechanism that allows them to cope with external pressures like any other type of productive organization.

Financial constraints, gender and start-ups. Finally, in Chapter 5 I have analysed the joint impact of gender and financial constraints on the formation of new business. As mentioned above, this study attempts to reconcile the findings of the empirical literature on women-led companies where there is no clear evidence on whether the gender of the owner enhances the eventual finance constraints the company may suffer from. My theoretical approach is the following: first, I hypothesize that financial constraints are much more important in the start-up stage for female owners, rather than in the later stage when the firm is set up and is operating. This implies that the reasons why the literature has not been able to identify gender effects is because they have only considered established companies. Second, I assume that in this case, the expectation that the generated surplus will be mostly appropriated by the financial institution (because of the potentially unfavourable credit conditions) is sufficient to deter potential applicants from seeking external funding. In other words, financial constraints appear not only to affect directly the number of start-ups by women, but more importantly the perception women have about how difficult it is to get external funding. Consistently with these two hypotheses, I have estimated three models of self-employment choice where gender and measures of financial constraints affect in different ways the individual's self-employment choice. Also I have used the English Household Survey on Entrepreneurship, 2003, that focuses on the individuals' intentions of setting up a new firm. The three models differ in the way gender and financial constraints affect the self-employment choice. Indeed, in the first model I assume that being financially constrained may affect directly the individual's self-employment choice and therefore in this model I am interested to test whether being female and/or from a minority background may enhance the impact of financial constraints on self-employment. In the second model, I assume that gender and/or the applicants' ethnic background affects the probability an individual has of being financially constrained; I also assume that only individuals who do not experience financial constraints may then set up their own firm. Finally, in the third model, I assume that gender and/or ethnic background can affect an individual's probability of seeking external funding and only individuals that are successful in this respect can then go for self-employment. The key findings from the models are quite supportive of my initial hypotheses. Indeed, I find that being female and/or of a minority background does not enhance the financial constraints that adversely impact the self-employment choice. On the contrary, as it would be expected, these are compounded by the lack of collateral and by the location. These results do not hide the possibility that women (of any ethnic background) may simply not opt for self-employment for reasons other than financial constraints. Indeed, in our models both gender and the ethnic background does not affect the self-employment choice per se, implicitly suggesting that the willingness of setting up a new firm is randomly distributed between the two sexes. Also, in our data, a self-selection mechanism is at work where women (of any ethnic background) decide not to seek external finance (as they may expect to encounter substantial financial constraints) and so implicitly decide not to be self-employed. Finally, from our data it seems that being located in a very deprived area does not affect the probability of becoming self-employed. These points together suggest that women in the general population perceive the existence of stronger financial barriers to business start-ups than men, and this may be discouraging them from seeking external financial support for business start-ups. I do not find evidence, however, that where females do seek finance for start-up they are any less likely to obtain it than males. This is suggestive of a dominant demand rather than supply-side effect. In either case, however, the aggregate effect is similar – that gender differences in access to finance are reducing female start-up rates.

From a policy perspective the key points from this study are that female start-up rates are being reduced by (a) the general perception of stronger financial barriers to start-up among females, and (b) their unwillingness to seek external finance for business start-ups. Addressing these issues is likely to require a combination of measures designed both to redress the perception that it is more difficult for females to access business finance and to encourage potential female entrepreneurs to be more ambitious in seeking external finance. Successfully addressing these issues alone will not, however, fully close the gap between male and female start-up rates as our data suggest there exists a further gender gap that cannot only be explained in terms of financial shortages. One of the key issues highlighted in the literature review was the longer-term dynamic effects of under-capitalization – the result of finance shortages – on the performance of female-owned firms. The data analysed here are purely cross-sectional, however, and while this makes it possible to draw some inferences about the effects on start-up rates, for example, it is impossible to draw implications about any impacts on the subsequent success of those start-up companies. Similarly, it proved difficult from the existing survey data to draw any firm conclusions about the impact of finance shortages on subsequent business performance. Both require more longitudinal follow-up of individuals that have participated in cross-sectional surveys and this could be considered as a research priority going forwards.

My main point is that the current literature tends to overemphasize the role that financial constraints play in affecting the growth and the performance of women-led companies once they are established. However, our analysis shows that financial constraints can have other effects and can interact with gender at an early stage as they generate the expectation that women suffer from future financial constraints. From a policy perspective this means that some effort must be put to affect the perception women have on the criteria used by financial institutions to allocate loans. However, it is also important policy-makers try to redress the balance between lenders and borrowers in the case of funding for female start-ups. Addressing these issues is likely to require a combination of measures designed both to redress the perception that it is more difficult for females to access business finance and to encourage potential female entrepreneurs to be more ambitious in seeking external finance.

This book also generates some general results that may be useful to both academics and policy-makers. From the studies contained in Chapters 3 and 4, it is possible to state that the economic performance (here considered in a very broad sense) can be improved thanks to increasing financial constraints. If this is the case, can policy-makers use potential financial constraints as policy instruments that induce firms to improve their performance? To answer this question, it is important to consider two issues. First, from the analysis it is clear that financial constraints can have a differential impact on economic outcomes if considered either ex ante or ex post. Ex ante, economic agents tend to internalize the possibility that they can experience financial constraints and this may influence their choices. The relationship between gender, finance constraints and self-employment is rather eloquent in this respect. Indeed, just the expectation (more or less justified) of future financial constraints can be sufficient to stop women from asking for external funds and then starting a new company. Ex post, the tightening of financial constraints can give economic agents the incentives to change their economic behaviour in such a way that economic outcomes (in our case, technical efficiency) can be influenced positively but only if they affect the distribution of rents. Indeed, when this is not the case, obviously the increasing financial pressure can either have no impact on the agents' behaviour or have undesirable effects. Second, policies to try to reduce the impact of financial constraints in the economic system must consider this differential impact. Indeed, in the first case, it is important to work on the perception economic agents have on how credit is allocated and what criteria financial institutions use to this end besides trying to relax the credit constraints altogether. In the second case, financial pressure may be beneficial to the firm as it pushes managers and workers to align their interests to those of the firm. Therefore, in this respect, the role of the policy-makers in alleviating the financial constraints should be rather limited as these should be allowed to work as a disciplining mechanism for the several constituencies that make up the firm. Third, the results from the studies suggest that there may be a potential non-linearity in the relationship between technical efficiency and financial constraints. Although it is not formalized, there is clearly a different reaction to financial constraints between firms that are on the frontier (i.e. firms that do not have any organizational slack) and firms that are not. Indeed, firms on the frontier that are exposed to intense financial pressure may need to reduce their investment and production activities in order to cope with the worsening of the financial pressure. In this case, policy measures must be aimed at relaxing the credit constraints altogether as firms do not have organizational slack to deal with the increasing financial pressure.

In sum, understanding how financial constraints work still poses interesting challenges. This book has suggested a different understanding of how financial constraints affect economic outcomes, with the main point being that financial constraints can generate additional effects that are not entirely predictable or undesirable. This way, I hope this study will serve as a foundation for a more complete understanding of the role financial constraints can play in the economic system.

Appendix A

This appendix lists the 3-digit sectors belonging to the four Pavitt sectors (High-tech, Specialized Supplier, Scale-intensive sector and Supplier-dominated sector) as provided by Capitalia.

High-tech sectors

256 Chemistry
257 Pharmaceuticals

330 Hardware
344 Electronics
364 Aeroplanes

Specialized supplier sectors

246 Abrasive materials
255 Inks
259 Other chemicals
321 Tools for agriculture
322 Tools for metals
323 Machinery for textiles
324 Machinery for food processing
325 Machinery for extractive processes
326 Transmission
327 Machinery for wood industry
328 Precision tools
348 Reparation of electronic machinery
371 Precision tools
372 Machinery for surgery
373 Photographic instruments
374 Clocks
482 Tyres
483 Plastic products
491 Jewellery
492 Musical instruments
493 Cinematographic laboratories
494 Toys
495 Other manufacturing industries
496 Clothing

Scale-intensive sectors

221 Steel-processing industries
222 Steel pipe production
223 Steel
224 Production of non-ferrous metals
242 Cement
243 Concrete
247 Glass
248 Pottery
251 Basic chemicals
258 Soap
260 Artificial fibres
341 Electric fibres

342 Motors
343 Electric tools for transport systems
345 TV set production
346 Domestic appliances
347 Electric tools for illumination
351 Construction of autovehicles
352 Vehicle body shell manufacturing
353 Accessories for autovehicles
361 Shipbuilding
362 Railways
363 Moto-cycles
365 Other transportation tools
420 Sugar
471 Paper
472 Paper transformation
473 Printing
474 Publishing
481 Rubber

Supplier-dominated sectors

211 Extraction of ferrous minerals
212 Extraction of non-ferrous minerals
231 Extraction of other material
232 Extraction of calcium
233 Extraction of salt
239 Extraction of other minerals
241 Production of materials for construction industry
244 Amianthus
245 Stone
311 Metallurgy
312 Semi-treatment of metals
313 Treatment of metals
314 Carpentery in metals
315 Heaters
316 Metal tools
319 Rest of mechanical sector
411 Animal and vegetable fats production
412 Meat processing firms
413 Milk processing firms
414 Fruit conservation
415 Fish conservation
416 Bird seeds
417 Pasta
418 Flour products

419 Bread
421 Chocolate
422 Food products for animals
423 Other food products
424 Alcohol
425 Wine
427 Beer
428 Mineral water
429 Tobacco
431 Wool
432 Cotton
433 Silk
434 Canapa
435 Jute
436 Wool products
437 Textiles
438 Rugs
439 Other textile products
441 Treatment of leather
442 Leather
451 Shoes
452 Hand-made shoes
453 Factory clothes production
454 Hand-made clothes
455 Other textile products
456 Furs
461 Wood
462 Half-finished wooden products
463 Carpentery
464 Wooden boxes
465 Other wood products
466 Cork
467 Wood furniture

Appendix B: the measurement of technical efficiency; the frontier approach

The frontier approach to the measurement of efficiency (both technical and allocative) is now an established tool available to both practitioners and policy-makers to evaluate the performance of productive units (Forsund and Hjalmarsson, 1979; Deprins *et al.*, 1984; Coelli and Perelman, 1986; Hughes, 1988; Perelman and Pestieu, 1988; Fecher, 1990; Fecher and Perelman, 1989; Fecher and Perelman, 1991; Fecher and Pestieu, 1991; Ferrier and Valdmanis, 1996; Grosskopf *et al.*, 1996; Coelli, 1997). The main reason for their success can be ascribed to both their consistency with the economic theory and their intuitive appeal. The approach is based on the notion that it is possible to compute for a sub-set of firms (or productive units in general) the best practice technology (called the "production frontier") that works as the standard against which it is possible to measure the efficiency of the units. This Appendix is devoted to the illustration of the analytical methods to the measurement of technical efficiency based on the notion of production frontier. There exists a rich literature that considers how to measure total factor productivity growth as well as by using frontier techniques (Caves *et al.*, 1982; Nishimizu and Page, 1982; Diewert, 1989; Fare *et al.*, 1989, 1992, 1993, 1994, 1995; Morrison and Diewert, 1990; Morrison, 1993). However, these techniques will not be considered in this Appendix for obvious space reasons.

I will start by defining the concept of technical efficiency and then I will illustrate the different techniques for the computation of the frontier first and of the efficiency scores afterwards. The concept of technical efficiency refers to the producer's ability to avoid wasting resources either by producing as much output as input usage allows, or by using as little input as output production allows. In other words, I can define technical efficiency as the adherence of the productive unit in question to its standard of optimality (given by the state of technology) (Fare and Lovell, 1978; Fried *et al.*, 1993; Fare *et al.*, 1994). The discrepancy between the effective capability of a productive unit to turn inputs into outputs and the relevant optimal standard measures the inefficiency of the unit. Historically, the measurement of technical efficiency has a long history, dating back to the Fifties and to the work of Koopmans (1953) first and Farrell (1957), afterwards. Koopmans provided a definition of what is referred to nowadays as technical efficiency: an input–output vector is technically efficient if, and only if, increasing any output (or decreasing any output) is possible only by decreasing some other input (or increasing some other output). This notion was, however, made operational by Farrell (1957), afterwards. He extended the work initiated by Koopmans and suggested that a useful way to measure technical efficiency is to consider inefficiency as the realized deviation from an idealized frontier isoquant. Production frontier serves as one such standard in the case of technical efficiency. The extent by which a firm lies below its production frontier, which sets the limit to the range of maximum obtainable output, can be regarded as a measure of inefficiency. More specifically, he proposed measuring technical inefficiency as 1 minus the equiproportionate reduction in all inputs that still allow continued production of given outputs. A score of unity indicates technical efficiency because no equiproportionate input reduction is feasible, and a score less than unity indicates the severity of technical efficiency. This measure is an input-oriented one; it is straightforward to convert this measure to the output-oriented one. In this case, the measure of the technical inefficiency is defined as 1 minus the equiproportionate expansion in output that still employs a given amount of inputs. Again, an index equal to 1 indicates technical efficiency while a score less than unity is a measure of technical inefficiency.

Let me define these measures formally, starting from the input-oriented one. Let producers use inputs $x = (x_1, ..., x_n) \in R_+^N$ to produce outputs $y = (y_1, ..., y_M) \in R_+^M$. Production technology can be then represented by the following input set:

$L(y) = x:(y,x)$ is feasible

which for every $y \in R_+^M$ has an isoquant:

$IsoqL(y) = x : x \in L(y), \lambda x \notin L(y), \lambda \in [0,1)$

and an efficient subset:

$EffL(y) = x : x \in L(y), x' \notin L(y), x' \le x,$

where x′ identifies all those input vectors below the production set and, there-fore, not belonging to the production set. The Farrell input-oriented measure of technical efficiency (DF$_i$) can now be given a somewhat more formal interpreta-tion in the following way:

$DF_i(y,x) = \min \lambda : \lambda x \in L(y) \le 1.$

The Farrell index is also the inverse of the Malmquist–Shepard distance func-tion, which measures the maximum amount by which an input vector can be shrunk along a ray while holding the output level constant.

Consider, now, the output-oriented measure of technical efficiency. Produc-tion technology can be represented with an output set P(x) where the output is feasible:

$P(x) = y:(x,y)$ is feasible.

For every $x \in R_+^N$ such output set has an isoquant:

$IsoqP(x) = y : y \in P(x), \theta y \notin P(x), \theta \in (1,\infty)$

and an efficient subset:

$EffP(x) = y : y \in P(x), y' \notin P(x), y' \ge y.$

The Debreu – Farrell output-oriented measure of technical efficiency (DF$_o$) is defined as:

$DF_o(x, y) = \max \theta : \theta y \in P(x) \le 1.$

However, the production possibility set that economic theory associates with any productive activity is an unknown. Therefore, the subsequent research has always dealt with the best way to identify the reference technology, that is the production possibilities set whose frontier is used to evaluate the observed productive activities (Grosskopf, 1986). Thus, the efficiency measurement literature may be roughly organized into two groups according to the methodology used to construct the reference technology: namely, it is customary to distinguish between parametric methods (including the deterministic approach of Aigner and Chu (1968) and the stochastic one of Aigner, Lovell and Schmidt (1977) and Jondrow *et al.* (1982)) and the non-parametric methods such as Data Envelopment Analysis (DEA, henceforth) described in Charnes, Cooper and Rhodes (1978).

The parametric methods express the frontier with a defined mathematical form. Aigner and Chu (1968) were the first to measure efficiency with a Cobb–Douglas production function, estimated by applying linear and quadratic programming algorithms. In this literature on the frontier regression model there are a number of further distinctions. The main one is between deterministic and stochastic frontiers. The former, linked to the names of Afriat (1972), Richmond (1974) and Gabrielsen (1975), assumes that the error term measures the technical inefficiency of the decision-making unit, sweeping away any other source of stochastic variation in the dependent variable. The stochastic specification of this model makes it unrealistic as it is not possible to assume that the only source of stochastic shocks to the frontier is inefficiency. Therefore, econometricians have largely abandoned the deterministic frontier as a useful model for efficiency measurement in favour of stochastic methods. These were first suggested by Aigner, Lovell and Schmidt (1977) and make a clear distinction between the statistical "noise" and inefficiency as such. Therefore the frontier is randomly placed by the whole collection of stochastic elements which might enter the model outside the control of the producer (see also Schmidt and Lovell, 1979; Stevenson, 1980; Waldman, 1982; Coelli, 1993). This simple cross-sectional stochastic model has also been extended to panel data models. Indeed, Pitt and Lee (1981), Schmidt and Sickles (1984), Battese and Coelli (1988, 1992), Battese *et al.* (1989), Kumbhakar (1990) and Cornwell, Schmidt and Sickles (1990) have derived efficiency scores (both fixed and time-variant) by stochastic production frontier models using panel data.

Assume there is a well-defined production structure, characterized by a smooth, continuous, continuously differentiable, quasi-concave production function. Producers are assumed to be price takers in their input markets, so input prices may be treated as exogenous. Consider producers using a vector of inputs $\mathbf{x}$ to produce a vector of outputs $\mathbf{y}$. If the vector of outputs can be aggregated in a scalar measure, the firm's technology can be represented by the following stochastic production function:

$$y_i = f(\mathbf{x}_i; \beta)\exp(u_i + v_i) \quad i = 1, \ldots, N, \tag{D1}$$

where β is a vector of technology parameters to be estimated. u_i represents the technical inefficiency entering the production model multiplicatively and assumed to be distributed independently of v_i and to satisfy the constraint $u_i < 0$ and v_i is the statistical error where i identify the producers, ranging from 1 to n. Consider a Cobb–Douglas functional form for (D1) and take the logs on both sides. Then (D1) becomes:

$$\ln y_i = \alpha + \beta \ln \mathbf{x_i} + u_i + v_i \; i = 1, \ldots, N. \tag{D2}$$

The econometric version of the output-oriented technical efficiency index is so given by:

$$TE_{io} = \exp(-u_i)|(u_i + v_i),$$

where the variables have been defined above. To compute the technical efficiency index it is necessary to estimate the production frontiers specified in (D2). The two available methods are the deterministic and the stochastic ones. The former assumes that the whole error term $u_i + v_i$ measures the technical inefficiency of the decision-making unit, sweeping away any other source of stochastic variation in the dependent variable. The estimators for deterministic frontiers are two: the Displaced Ordinary Least Squares (DOLS) and the Corrected Ordinary Least Squares (COLS) technique. The DOLS estimator was introduced by Richmond (1974). It estimates the production function by OLS and modifies the estimated OLS intercept with the estimated mean of u_i. The assumption concerning the structure of the stochastic error is pretty hard to justify and therefore this model has been left in favour of stochastic specifications first introduced by Aigner, Lovell and Schmidt (1977). The latter method disentangles the effect of the inefficiency term from the stochastic shock and tries to derive measures of technical efficiency net of stochastic shocks. Stochastic frontier models are due to Aigner, Lovell and Schmidt (1977): they assume that deviations from the production frontier might not be completely under the control of the agent being studied. Any particular producer faces her own production frontier which is randomly placed by the whole collection of stochastic elements entering the model outside the control of the producer. In this case, the Maximum Likelihood estimation is advised as the compound disturbance in this model, while asymmetrically distributed, is otherwise well behaved. The one-sided part of the compound disturbance (u_i) is assumed to be the absolute value of a Normally distributed variable, though several specifications have been considered, like the Gamma (Beckers and Hammond, 1987), Exponential and the Truncated distributions. The models presented so far allow one to derive the reference technology only for cross-sectional observations of productive units. One problem with cross-sectional data is that the technical efficiency indices cannot be separated from firm-specific effects which may not be related to the inefficiency. While this problem has been recognized long ago, it has been solved only since panel data have been available. The first model using panel data was first proposed by Schmidt and Sickles (1984); afterwards, alternative specifications have been suggested by Pitt and Lee (1981), Schmidt and

Sickles (1984), Battese and Coelli (1988, 1992), Cornwell, Schmidt and Sickles (1990), and Kumbhakar (1990).

Schmidt and Sickles (1984) specified a production frontier model of panel data as:

$$\ln y_{it} = \alpha + \beta \ln \mathbf{x}_{it} + u_i + v_{it} \, i = 1, \ldots, N \, t = 1, \ldots, T, \tag{D3}$$

where the variables have been defined above. Notice that now both outputs and inputs can vary across time and producers, unlike before. In this model, statistical noise varies over producers and time, but technical inefficiency varies only over producers. The firm-specific inefficiency can be merged with the constant to obtain conventional panel data model in which there is no time effect and the firm effect is one-sided. In this case estimation of (D3) does not require an assumption on the functional form of the firm effects u_i and if there are no time-invariant inputs it is not necessary to assume that u_i is distributed independently of the inputs.

Schmidt and Sickles consider three ways of estimating (D3). If the u_i are treated as firm-specific constants, the model may be estimated by the Fixed Effect estimator. In this case, estimates of the individual effects are extracted as follows: the estimator produces either a set of firm-specific constants α_i and therefore the inefficiency component can be computed as follows:

$$\hat{u}_i = \hat{\alpha}_i - \max(\hat{\alpha}_i).$$

By construction, one of the firms meets the benchmark value and the remaining firms have positive inefficiency estimates. This approach has the distinctive advantage that it dispenses with the assumption that the firm inefficiencies are uncorrelated with the input levels. Moreover, no assumption of Normality of residuals is needed. However, if the assumption of independence of the inefficiencies and input levels can be maintained, then a random effect estimator might be preferable. In this case (D3) can be estimated with a Generalized Least Squares estimator. An estimate of the inefficiency component can be derived as:

$$\hat{u}_i = \hat{u}_i - \max(\hat{u}_i).$$

One of the main shortcomings in the aforesaid approach is that the ranks of the firms in terms of efficiencies remain unchanged over time and the relationship is constrained to be monotonic over time. Several approaches have been suggested to solve this problem (see Battese and Coelli (1988, 1992); Cornwell *et al.* (1990); Kumbhakar (1990)). Among the suggested models, the most used is the one suggested by Battese and Coelli (1992). They suggested a specification of (D2) where technical efficiency is allowed to vary over time (with the possibility of testing the time invariance) and the MLE techniques are used. More specifically, they proposed a stochastic production model for (un)balanced panel data with firm effects assumed to be distributed as truncated normal random variables and permitted to vary systematically with time. The model may be expressed as:

$$\ln y_{it} = \alpha + \beta \ln \mathbf{x_{it}} + u_{it} + v_{it} \; i = 1, \ldots, N \; t = 1, \ldots, T,$$

where the variables are those defined above. This time, however, u_{it} is allowed to vary across producers and time. v_{it} are random variables which are assumed to be iid $N(0, \sigma_v^2)$ and independent of u_{it} where this is equal to $u_i \exp(-\varepsilon(t-T))$ where u_i are the non-negative random variables which are assumed to account for technical inefficiency in production and are assumed to be iid as truncations at zero of the $N(\mu, \sigma_u^2)$; ε is a parameter to be estimated.

The Battese and Coelli (1995) model is an extension of Battese and Coelli (1992). The main feature is that it allows us to specify the determinants of the distribution of efficiency across the observations and to estimate their impact on the scores. In this model, the production frontier specification includes a composed error term:

$$\varepsilon_{it} = u^{it} - v^{it},$$

allowing for both firm-specific inefficiency effects, u^{it} and a stochastic noise v^{it} distributed as a $N(0, \sigma_v^2)$. The u^{it} reflects the shortfall of the firms relative to their own best practice in each period, where the best practice for the firm is determined by the frontier. The technical efficiency term is comprised of non-negative random variables that are assumed to be independently distributed as truncations of the $N(\delta z_{it}, \sigma_u^2)$ distribution, where z_{it} are the factors that may influence the mean inefficiency in our sample of firms and δ is a vector of parameters to be estimated. The production frontier is estimated using Maximum Likelihood, as in Battese and Coelli (1995). The firm-level technical efficiency score is then computed as:

$$TE^{it} = \exp(-\hat{u}_{it}).$$

Data Envelopment Analysis

The non-parametric approach to the construction of productive frontiers and the measurement of efficiency goes by the descriptive title of Data Envelopment Analysis (DEA), due to Charnes *et al.* (1978). They do not posit any explicit relationship between the observations and the frontier and construct the production frontier from the observed input–output ratios by linear programming technique. They are non-statistical as no assumption about the stochastic properties of the data is required. The main feature of the non-parametric methods is that they are deterministic, that is they do not allow for stochastic noise. So the measured technical efficiency scores can be a mix of both technical inefficiency and stochastic shocks to the technology. Suppose producers use input vector $\mathbf{x}$ to produce the output vector **y**. To measure technical efficiency, weights are attached to each producer's inputs and outputs in order to solve the problem:

$$\min_{u,v} = \frac{v^T x_0}{u^T y_0} \tag{D4}$$

subject to:

$$\frac{v^T x_i}{u^T y_i} \le 1 \; i = 1,..I \text{ and } u,v < 0.$$

where x_0, y_0 is the input–output vector of the producer being evaluated, (x_i, y_i) is the input–output vector of the i-th producer in the sample and v^T and u^T are weights attached to each producer. The problem is to derive a set of non-negative weights minimizing the weighted input-to-output ratio for the producer being evaluated, subject to the constraint that no producer in the sample has a ratio less than unity. This non-linear ratio model can be converted to the linear programming "multiplier" problem:

$$\min_{u,v} v^T x_o \tag{D5}$$

subject to:

$$u^T y_o = 1$$
$$v^T x_i \le u^T y_i$$

$$i = 1, ..., I$$

$$u, v \le 0.$$

Its dual is the linear programming "envelopment" problem:

$$\max_{\theta, \lambda} \theta \tag{D6}$$

subject to:

$$X\lambda \le x_0$$
$$\theta y_o \le Y\lambda$$
$$\lambda \le 0$$

where X is an n by I input matrix with columns x_i, Y is an m by I output matrix with columns y_i and λ is an I by 1 intensity vector. In the DEA problem the performance of a producer is evaluated in terms of his ability to expand its output vector subject to the constraints imposed by best observed practice. If radial expansion is possible for a producer, its optimal θ is larger than 1, while if radial expansion is not possible, its optimal θ is equal to 1.

The DEA problem (D4) is an output-oriented one. It is simple to obtain an analogous input-oriented envelopment problem by replacing (D4) with a maximization problem, (D5) with a maximization multiplier problem and (D6) with a minimization envelopment problem. The DEA model above is known as the CCR model after Charnes *et al.* (1978). This model imposes two restrictions on frontier technology, those are constant returns-to-scale and strong disposability of inputs and outputs. Constant returns-to-scale is the restriction that is most commonly relaxed. Non-increasing returns-to-scale is modelled by adding to (D6) the constraint:

$$e^T \lambda \leq 1,$$

where e is a vector of ones. Variable returns-to-scale is modelled by adding to (D6) the constraint $e^T \lambda = 1$. The variable returns-to-scale formulation is frequently referred to as the BCC model after Banker *et al.* (1984).

Notes

1 Introduction

1 The specific policy measures change across countries. However, generally speaking, such schemes tend to include the creation of loan funds, group lending mechanisms, and establishing new relationships with conventional lenders through loan guarantee programmes and initial screening programmes (Weiss, 1990).

2 Credit constraints and economic outcomes: a short survey

1 For very good surveys, see Bernanke, 1993, Hubbard, 1995 and Schiantarelli, 1996.
2 Stiglitz and Weiss first, and Williamson afterwards, have examined the characteristics of the credit market equilibrium when it is affected by adverse selection and moral hazard with costly monitoring respectively.
3 Indeed, it is important to remember that credit constraints are quite pervasive and therefore affect not only firms but consumers as well.
4 Among others, see Fazzari *et al.*, 1988 for an analysis of the relationship between the within-firm variation in physical investment and internal finance in a panel of US manufacturing firms. Hoshy *et al.*, 1991 and Devereux and Schiantarelli, 1989 offer the same kind of evidence for Japanese and British firms, respectively.
5 In this section, it is not my purpose to explain in detail the different models of the demand for investment. To this purpose, useful surveys are those by Schiantarelli, 1996 and by Schaller, 1993.
6 This is based on the assumption that expected earnings can proxy for expected utility.
7 However, this finding can simply derive from problems of reverse causality.
8 In a study conducted by Hisrich and Brush (1982), 53 percent of the respondents invested less than US$5,000 at the start-up phase of the company.
9 SBS (2004) *Annual Small Business Survey: Executive Summary*, SBS: Sheffield.
10 A belief typically found by researchers during the 1980s (Pellegrino and Reece, 1982; Hisrich and Brush, 1984), but similar results have been reported as recently as 1999 (Anna *et al.*, 1999).
11 Orser *et al.* (1994) and Koper (1993) have reported similar results.
12 However, Haines *et al.* (1999) found no significant gender difference in the industry in which the businesses operated among firms that secured loans.

3 Technical efficiency and finance constraints: an empirical analysis for Italian manufacturing, 1989–1994

1 The sufficient condition is that $a > -\gamma \bar{k}_{i,t+1}$.
2 See Appendix A for the division of firms from Italian manufacturing across the four Pavitt sectors, according to the Capitalia database, 1997.

3 Interested readers should consult Battese and Coelli (1995) for a comprehensive analysis of the approach. Also, a brief survey of the frontier methods is presented in Appendix D.

4 These are also known as inefficiency effects.

5 The estimation has been carried out by using Frontier version 4.1. This is a FORTRAN program created and provided by Tim Coelli, University of Queensland, Australia. The program is compiled using a Lahey F77LEM/32 compiler for an IBM-compatible PC. This program provides maximum likelihood estimates of a wide variety of stochastic frontier production and cost functions.

6 This has been computed as in Kumbhakar and Lovell, 2000.

7 By small and medium-sized firm it is meant a firm with less than 250 employees, consistent with the European Commission directive of 23/7/1996.

8 There are about 200 questions in the 4th and 5th survey, while the 8th survey contains 400 questions.

4 Product market competition, financial pressure and producers' cooperatives

1 See also Hay and Liu (1997) for a discussion on this point.

2 The computation of the DEA model has been carried out by using the software Deap version 2.1 provided by Tim Coelli.

3 The firms classified in this sector include firms that both grow and process grapes to produce wine. For the remainder of the paper, I will refer to this sector interchangeably as the wine sector or wine industry. The panel is not balanced as a company should satisfy the size limit that operating revenue is equal to at least 1 million euros to be included in the database.

4 More information on this database can be found at www.bvdep.com/browse5.asp.

5 The data set gives no information on firm output mix: firms could be specialized in the high end or low end of the market or they can produce both types of products. However, generally cooperatives produce less higher quality wine than traditional firms even if they are recently trying to produce more higher quality wine than in the past (ISMEA, 2002).

6 It was 55 per cent in 1996 (van Bekkum and van Dijk, 1998).

7 The critical values for the test that $\gamma = 0$ are obtained from Table 1 of Kodde and Palm (1986) where the degrees of freedom are q + 1 where q is the number of parameters assumed equal to zero, but are not boundary values.

8 There is neither evidence of embodied technical progress since the LR test of the translog specification with embodied technical progress against the actual specification is equal to 2.4 with number of restrictions equal to 4 (against a critical value of 9.5 at a 5 per cent significance level). The specification, with 4 dummy variables for each year, used to detect the presence of discontinuous technical progress, has also been rejected on the basis of the LR test equal to 0.16.

5 Self-employment and gender: how important are financial constraints?

1 In the remainder of this chapter I will use "entrepreneur" and "self-employed" as synonyms.

2 The assumption is the individuals with a degree have a potential for a higher income and therefore the opportunity cost of becoming self-employed is higher.

3 The same assumption as specified in the footnote 33 applies here.

4 SBS (2004) *SBS Household Survey of Entrepreneurship, 2003* (by NOP Social and Political), SBS: Sheffield.

5 Although one interesting finding in the survey is that many black people are Thinkers (31 per cent) that do not follow through to become Doers.

References

Acemoglu, D. (1998), "Credit market imperfections and separation of ownership from control", *Journal of Economic Theory*, volume 78, pp. 355–381.

Afriat, S. (1972) "Efficiency estimation of production functions", *International Economic Review* 13: 3, October, 568–598.

Aghion, P., Bloom, N., Blundell, R., Griffith, R. and Howitt, P. (2003) Competition and Innovation: An Inverted U Relationship, NBER Working Paper no. 9269.

Aghion, P. and Griffith, R. (2005) *Competition and Growth. Reconciling Theory and Evidence*, MIT Press, Cambridge, MA.

Aghion, P. and Howitt, P. (1998) *Endogenous Growth Theory*, MIT Press.

Aigner, D.J. and Chu, S.F. (1968) On estimating the industry production function, *American Economic Review* 58: 4, 826–839.

Aigner, D.J., Lovell, C.A.K. and Schmidt, P.J. (1977) "Formulation and estimation of stochastic frontier production function models", *Journal of Econometrics*, 6: 1, 21–37.

Akerlof, G. (1970) "The market for lemons: qualitative uncertainty and the market mechanism", *Quarterly Journal of Economics* 84: 3, 488–500.

Aldrich, H. (1989) "Networking among women entrepreneurs", in Hagan, O., C. Rivchun, C. and Sexton D. (eds) (1989) *Women-owned Businesses*. New York *et al.*: Praeger, 103–132.

Amemiya, T. and Macurdy, T.E. (1986) "Instrumental variable of an error component model", *Econometrica*, 54, 869–881.

Anna, A.L., Chandler, G.N., Jansen, E. and Mero, N.P. (1999) "Women business owners in traditional and non-traditional industries", *Journal of Business Venturing*, 15, 279–303.

Apilado, V. and Millington, J. (1992) "Restrictive loan covenants and risk adjustment in small business lending," *Journal of Small Business Management* 30(1), 38–48.

Arenius, P. and Autio, E., (2006), "Financing of small businesses: are Mars and Venus more alike than different?", *Venture Capital* 8(2), 93–107.

Balestra, P. and Nerlove, M. (1966) "Pooling cross section and time series data in the estimation of a dynamic model: the demand for natural gas", *Econometrica* 34, 585–612.

Baltagi, B. (2001) *Econometric Analysis of Panel Data* (Second Edition), New York: Wiley.

Banca d'Italia (1997) Relazione Generale, Roma, Italy.

Banker, R.D., Charnes, A. and Cooper, W.W. (1984) "Some models for estimating technical and scale inefficiencies in Data Envelopment Analysis", *Management Sciences* 30: 9, 1078–1092.

Bartlett, W., Cable, J., Estrin, S., Jones, D. and Smith, S. (1992) "Labor-managed cooperatives and private firms in North Central Italy: an empirical comparison", *Industrial and Labor Relations Review*, 46(1), 103–118.

Bates, T. (1991) "Commercial bank financing of white- and black-owned small business start-ups", *Quarterly Review of Economics and Business* 31(1), 64–80.

Battese, G.E. and Coelli, T.J. (1988) "Prediction of firm-level technical efficiencies with a generalised frontier production function and panel data", *Journal of Econometrics* 38, 387–399.

Battese, G.E. and Coelli, T.J. (1992) "Frontier production functions, technical efficiency and panel data with application to paddy farmers in India", *Journal of Productivity Analysis* 3, 153–169.

Battese, G.E. and Coelli, T.J. (1995) "A model for technical efficiency effects in a stochastic frontier production function for panel data", *Empirical Economics* 20, 325–332.

Battese, G.E., Coelli, T.J. and Colby, T.C. (1989) "Estimation of frontier production functions and the efficiencies of Indian farms using panel data from ICRISAT's village level studies", *Journal of Quantitative Economics* 5, 327–348.

Beaudry, P. and Poitevin, M. (1995) "Competitive screening in financial markets when borrowers can recontract", *Review of Economic Studies* 62, 401–423.

Belcourt, M., Burka, R. and Lee-Gosselin, H. (1991) "The Glass Box: Women business owners in Canada", Canadian Advisory Council on the Status of Women, Government of Canada.

Berger, A.N. and Udell, G.F. (2002) "Small business credit availability and relationship lending: The importance of bank organizational structure", *Economic Journal* 112, 32–53.

Bernanke, B. (1983) "Non-monetary effects of the financial crisis in the propagation of the Great Depression", *American Economic Review* 73, 257–276.

Bernanke, B. and Gertler, M. (1989) "Agency costs, net worth and business fluctuations", *American Economic Review* 79: 1, 14–31.

Bernanke, B. and Gertler, M. (1990) "Financial fragility and economic performance", *Quarterly Journal of Economics* 105, 87–114.

Besanko, D. and Thakor, A.V. (1987) "Collateral and rationing: sorting equilibria in monopolistic and competitive credit markets", *International Economic Review* 28, 671–689.

Bester, H. (1987) "The role of collateral in credit market with imperfect information", *European Economic Review* 31, 887–899.

Bhargava, A. (1991) "Identification and panel data models with endogenous regressors", *Review of Economic Studies* 58, 129–140.

Bianchi, S.M. (2000) "Maternal employment and time with children: dramatic change or surprising continuity?", *Demography*, 37, 401–414.

Birgegaard, Lars E. and Genberg, Bjorn (1994) Cooperative Adjustment in a Changing Environment in Sub-Saharan Africa, ICA Document, Geneve, Switzerland.

Blair M. (1995) *Ownership and Control: Rethinking Corporate Governance for the Twentieth Century*, Washington, DC: Brookings Institute.

Blair M. (1999) "Firm-specific human capital and theories of the firm", in M. Blair and M. Roe (eds) *Employees and Corporate Governance*, Washington, DC: Brookings Institute.

Blanchard, O.J., Rhee, C. and Summers, L. (1993) "The stock market, profit and investment", *Quarterly Journal of Economics*, 108, 125–134.

Blanchflower, D.G. and Oswald, A.J. (1998) "What makes an entrepreneur?" *Journal of Labor Economics* 16, 26–60.

Blanchflower, D.G. (2000) "Self-employment in OECD countries", *Labour Economics* 7, 471–505.

Bond, S. and Meghir, C. (1994) "Dynamic investment models and the firm's financial policy", *Review of Economic Studies* 61, 197–222.

Bonin, J., Jones, D.C. and Putterman, L. (1993) "Theoretical and empirical studies of producer cooperatives: will ever the twain meet?" *Journal of Economic Literature*, 31(3), 1290–1320.

Boot, A.W.A. and Thakor, A.V. (1994) "Moral hazard and secured lending in an infinitely repeated market game", *International Economic Review* 35(4), 899–920.

Boot, A.W.A., Thakor, A.V. and Udell, G.F. (1991) "Secured lending and default risk: equilibrium analysis, policy implication and empirical results", *Economic Journal*, 101(3), 458–72.

Borjas, G. and Bronars, S. (1989) "Consumer discrimination and self-employment", *Journal of Political Economy* 97, 581–605.

Bornheim, S.P. and Herbeck, T.H. (1998) "A research note on the theory of SME–bank relationships", *Small Business Economics* 10 4: 327–331.

Brau, J.C. (2002) "Do banks price owner-manager agency costs? An examination of small business borrowing", *Journal of Small Business Management* 140(4), 273–286.

Bruce, D. (2000) "Effects of the United States tax system on transitions into self-employment", *Labour Economics* 7, 545–574.

Bruni, A., Gherardi, S. and Poggio, B. (2005) *Gender and Entrepreneurship: An Ethnographical Approach* Abingdon and New York: Routledge.

Brush, C.G. and Hisrich, R. (1991) "Antecedent influences on women-owned businesses", *Journal of Managerial Psychology* 6, 9–16.

Buttner, E.H. and Rosen, B. (1989) "Funding new business ventures: are decision makers biased against women entrepreneurs", *Journal of Business Venturing* 4(4), 249–261.

Buttner, E.H. and Rosen, B. (1992) "Rejection in the loan application process: male and female entrepreneurs' perceptions and subsequent intentions", *Journal of Small Business Management* 30(1), 58–65.

Caballero, R. and Hammour, M. (1994) "The cleansing effect of recessions", *American Economic Review* 84(5), 1350–1368.

Caballero, R. and Hammour, M. (1996) "The fundamental transformation in macroeconomics", *American Economic Review* Papers and Proceedings 86(2).

Cable, J. and Wilson, N., (1989) "Profit-sharing and productivity: an analysis of UK engineering firms", *Economic Journal* 99, 366–375.

Cahuc P. and Dormont, B. (1997) "Does profit-sharing increase productivity and employment? A theoretical model and empirical evidence on French micro data", *Labour Economics* 4, 293–319.

Calomiris, C.W. and Hubbard, R.G. (1989) "Price flexibility, credit availability and economic fluctuations: evidence from the United States, 1894–1909", *Quarterly Journal of Economics* 104: 3, 429–452.

Calomiris, C.W. and Hubbard, R.G. (1990) "Firm heterogeneity, internal finance and Credit Rationing", *Economic Journal* 100: 1, 90–104.

Carter, S. and Cannon, T. (1992) *Women as Entrepreneurs*, London: Academic Press.

Carter, S. and Rosa, P. (1998) "The financing of male- and female-owned businesses", *Entrepreneurship and Regional Development* 10 (3): 225–241.

Carter, S., Anderson, S. and Shaw, E. (2001) Women's business ownership: a review of the academic, popular and internet literature, Report to the Small Business Service, Sheffield.

Carter, S., Anderson, S. and Shaw, E. (2004) "Women's business ownership: a review of the academic, popular and internet literature with a UK policy focus", in *EFMD, ARPENT: Annual Review of Progress in Entrepreneurship Research*, Brussels: EFMD.

Casper, L.M. and O'Connell, M. (1998) "Work, income, the economy, and married fathers as child-care providers", *Demography* 35, 243–250.

Cavalluzzo, K.S., Cavalluzzo, L.C. and Wolken, J.D. (2002) "Competition, small business financing, and discrimination: evidence from a new survey", *Journal of Business* 75(4), 641–679.

Caves, D., Christensen, L. and Diewert, W.E. (1982) "The economic theory of index numbers and the measurement of input, output and productivity", *Econometrica* 50(6), 1393–1414.

Centre for Women's Business Research (2004) *Women-owned Business in the US: Trends in the U.S. and 50 States*, Centre for Women's Business Research: Washington, DC.

Chaganti, R. and Parasuraman, S. (1996) "A study of the impacts of gender on business performance and management patterns in small businesses", *Entrepreneurship Theory and Practice* 21(2), 73–75.

Chaganti, R., DeCarolis, D. and Deeds, D. (1995) "Predictors of capital structure in small ventures, *Entrepreneurship Theory and Practice* 20(2), 7–18.

Chamberlain, G. (1982) "Multivariate regression models for panel data", *Journal of Econometrics* 19, 5–46.

Chandler, G.N. and Hanks, S.H. (1998) "An examination of the substitutability of founders' human and financial capital in emerging business ventures", *Journal of Business Venturing* 13 (5), 353–369.

Charnes, A., Cooper, W.W. and Rhodes, E. (1978) "Measuring the efficiency of decision-making units", *European Journal of Operation Research* 2(6), 429–444.

Chirinko, R.S. (1987) "Tobin's q and financial policy", *Journal of Monetary Economics* 19, 189–201.

Chirinko, R.S. (1993) "Business fixed investment spending", *Journal of Economic Literature* 31, 1214–1256.

Chirinko, R. and Schaller, H. (1995) "Why does liquidity matter in investment equations", *Journal of Money, Credit and Banking* 27, 527–548.

Coelli, T.J. (1993) Finite Sample Properties of Stochastic Frontier Estimators and Associated Test Statistics, WPEAS, 70, University of New England, Australia.

Coelli, T.J. (1997) A Multi-Stage Methodology for the Solution of Orientated ED Models, mimeo.

Coelli, T. (2003) An Analysis of Technical Efficiency in Australian Coal-Fired Generation Plants, University of Queensland.

Coelli, T.J. and Perelman, S. (1996) Efficiency Measurement, Multiple-Output Technologies and Distance Functions: with Application to European Railways, CREPP, 5, University of Liege, Belgium.

Cole, R.A. and Wolken, J.D. (1995) "Financial services used by small businesses: evidence from the 1993 national survey of small business finances", *Federal Reserve Bulletin*, July, 629–666.

Coleman, S. (2000) "Access to capital and terms of credit: a comparison of men- and women-owned small businesses", *Journal of Small Business Management* 38(3), 37–52.

Coleman, S. and Carsky, M. (1996) "Financing small business: strategies employed by women entrepreneurs", *Journal of Applied Management and Entrepreneurship* 3(1), 28–42.

Connelly, R. (1992) "Self-employment and providing child care", *Demography* 29, 17–29.

Cornwell, C., Schmidt, P. and Sickles, R.C. (1990) "Production frontiers with cross-sectional and time-series variation in efficiency levels", *Journal of Econometrics* 46(1/2), 185–200.

Cosh, A. and Hughes, A. eds (2003) *Enterprise Challenged: Policy and Performance in the British SME Sector 1999–2002*, Cambridge: ESRC Centre for Business Research.

Cressy, R. and Toivanen, O. (2001) "Is there adverse selection in the credit market?" *Venture Capital* 3, 215–238.

Curran, J. and Blackburn, R. (1993) Enterprise and the High St Bank, Small Business Research Centre, Kingston Business School, Kingston University.

Darian, J.C. (1975) "Convenience of work and the job constraint of children", *Demography* 12, 245–258.

De Meza, D. and Webb, D.C. (1987) "Too much investment in problems of asymmetric information", *Quarterly Journal of Economics* 102, 281–292.

Deprins, D., Simar, L. and Tulkens, H. (1984) "Measuring labour-efficiency in post offices", in M. Marchand, P. Pestieu and H. Tulkens (eds) *The Performance of Public Enterprises: Concepts and Measurement*, North-Holland.

Devereux, M. and Schiantarelli, F. (1989) Investment, Financial Factors and Cash-Flow: Evidence from UK Panel Data, NBER Working Paper, 3116.

Devine, T. (1994) "Changes in wage-and-salary returns to skill and the recent rise in female self employment", *American Economic Review* 84, 108–113.

Diewert, W.E. (1989) The Measurement of Productivity, DP n.89–04, Department of Economics, University of British Columbia.

Duchenaut, B. (1997) Women Entrepreneurs in SMEs. Report prepared for the OECD Conference on Women Entrepreneurs in Small and Medium Sized Enterprises: A Major Force for Innovation and Job Creation (Paris, France: OECD).

Dunn, T. and Holtz-Eakin, D. (2000) "Financial capital, human capital, and the transition to self-employment: evidence from intergenerational links", *Journal of Labour Economics* 18, 282–305.

Edwards, L. and Field-Hendrey, E. (1996) "Home-based workers: data from the 1990 Census of Population", *Monthly Labour Review* 119(11), 26–34.

Ennew, C. and McKechnie, S. (1998) "The nature of the banking relationship: a comparison of the experiences of male and female small business owners", *International Small Business Journal* 16(3), 39–55.

Evans, D.S. and Jovanovic, B. (1989) "An estimated model of entrepreneurial choice under liquidity constraints", *Journal of Political Economy* 97, 808–827.

Evans, D.S. and Leighton, L.S. (1989) "Some empirical aspects of entrepreneurship", *American Economic Review* 79, 519–535.

Fabowale, L., Orser, B. and Riding, A. (1995) "Gender, structural factors, and credit terms between Canadian small businesses and financial institutions", *Entrepreneurship Theory and Practice* 19(4), 41–65.

Fairlie, R. and Meyer, B. (1996) "Ethnic and racial self-employment differences and possible explanations", *Journal of Human Resources* 31, 757–793.

Fan, W. and White, M.J. (2003) "Personal bankruptcy and the level of entrepreneurial activity", *Journal of Law and Economics* 46, 543–567.

Fare, R. and Lovell, K. (1978) "Measuring the technical efficiency of production", *Journal of Economic Theory* 19: 1, 150–162.

Fare, R., Grosskopf, S. and Kokkelenberg, E. (1989) "Measuring plant capacity, utilization and technical change: a nonparametric approach", *International Economic Review* 30(3), 655–666.

Fare, R., Grosskopf, S., Lindgren, B. and Roos, P. (1992) "Productivity in Swedish pharmacies: a Malmquist input index approach", *Journal of Productivity Analysis* 3(1/2), 270–285.

Fare, R., Grosskopf, S., Lindgren, B. and Roos, P. (1995) "Productivity developments in Swedish hospitals: a Malmquist output index approach", in A. Charnes, W.W. Cooper, A.Y. Lewin and L.M. Seiford (eds) *Data Envelopment Analysis: Theory, Methodology and Applications*, Boston: Kluwer, 253–272.

Fare, R., Grosskopf, S. and Lovell, C.A.K. (1994) *Production Frontiers*, New York: Cambridge University Press.

Fare, R., Grosskopf, S., Lovell, C.A.K. and Yaisawarng, S. (1993) "Derivation of shadow prices for undesirable outputs: a distance function approach", *Review of Economics and Statistics* 75, 374–380.

Fare, R., Grosskopf, S., Norris, M. and Zhang, Z. (1994) "Productivity growth, technical progress and efficiency changes in industrialised countries", *American Economic Review* 84, 66–83.

Farmer, R.E.A. (1985) "Implicit contracts with asymmetric information and bankruptcy: the effect of interest rates on layoffs", *Review of Economic Studies* 52, 427–442.

Farrell, M.J. (1957) "The measurement of productive efficiency", *Journal of the Royal Statistical Society*, Series A 120, 3, 253–290.

Fay, M. and Williams, L. (1993) "Gender bias and the availability of business loans", *Journal of Business Venturing* 8(4), 295–376.

Fazzari, S., Hubbard, R.G. and Petersen, B.C. (1988) "Financing constraints and corporate investment", *Brooking Papers on Economic Activity* 1, 141–195.

Fecher, F. (1990) Productivity Growth, Catching-Up and Innovation in OECD Manufacturing Sectors, paper presented at the 5th EEA Meeting, Lisbon.

Fecher, F. and Perelman, S. (1989) Productivity Growth, Technological Progress and RandD in OECD Industrial Activities, Public Finance and Steady Economic Growth, Proceedings of the 45th Congress of the International Institute of Public Finance, G. Krause-Junk, ed.

Fecher, F. and Perelman, S. (1991) Productivity Growth and Technical Efficiency in OECD Industrial Activities, University of Liège, Belgium.

Fecher, F. and Pestieu, P. (1991) Efficiency and Competition in Financial Services, presented at the CIRIEC Conference, University of Liège, Belgium.

Ferrantino, M., Ferrier, G.D. and Linvill, C.B. (1995) "Organizational form and efficiency: evidence from Indian sugar manufacturing", *Journal of Comparative Economics* 21(1), 29–53.

Ferrier, G.D. and Valdmanis, V. (1996) "Rural hospital performance and its correlates", *Journal of Productivity Analysis* 7:1, 63–80.

Fielden, S.L. and Dawe, A. (2004) "Entrepreneurship and social inclusion", *Women in Management Review* 19(3), 139–142.

Filippi, M. (2004) "Reorganisations dans la Cooperation Agricole: Proximites et Solidarite Territoriale", *Economie Rurale* v.0, 280. 42–58.

Fischer, E.M., Reuber, A.R. and Dyke, L.S. (1993) "A theoretical overview and extension of research on sex, gender and entrepreneurship", *Journal of Business Venturing* 8(8), 151–168.

Fischer, I. (1934) "Debt deflation theory of depression", *Econometrica* 337–357.

Forsund, F.R. and Hjalmarsson, L. (1979) "Frontier production functions and technical progress: a study of general milk production in Swedish plants", *Economic Journal* 89, 294–315.

Fraser, S. (2005) Finance for Small and Medium Sized Enterprises: A Report on the 2004 UK Survey of SME Finances, Warwick Business School: Coventry.

Fried, H.O., Lovell, C.A.K. and Schmidt, S. (eds.) (1993) *The Measurement of Productive Efficiency: Techniques and Applications*, New York: Oxford University Press.

Fujii, E.T. and Hawley, C.B. (1991) "Empirical aspects of self-employment", *Economics Letters* 36, 323–329.

Gabrielsen, A. (1975) On Estimating Efficient Production Functions, Working Paper, A-85, Department of Humanities and Social Sciences, Bergen.

Galizzi, G. (2000) Le caratteristiche strutturali dell'offerta dei prodotti agricoli, mimeo, Piacenza.

Gatewood, E., Carter, N.M., Brush, C.G., Greene, P.G. and Hart, M.M. (2003) Women Entrepreneurs, their Ventures and the Venture Capital Industry: An Annotated Bibliography (Stockholm: Entrepreneurship and Small Business Institute).

Gertler, M. (1988) "Financial structure and real economic activity", *Journal of Money, Credit and Banking* 20, 559–588.

Gertler, M. (1992) Financial capacity and output fluctuations in an economy with multiperiod financial relationships", *Review of Economic Studies* 59, 455–472.

Gertler, M. and Gilchrist, S. (1993) "The role of credit market imperfections in the monetary transmission mechanism: arguments and evidence", *Scandinavian Journal of Economics* 95: 1, 43–64.

Gertler, M. and Gilchrist, S. (1994) "Monetary policy, business cycles and the behaviour of small manufacturing firms", *Quarterly Journal of Economics* 109, 309–340.

Gertler, M. and Hubbard, R.G. (1988) Financial Factors in Business Fluctuations, NBER Working Paper, n. 2758.

Gertler, M.R., Hubbard, R.G. and Kashyap, A. (1991) "Interest rate spreads, credit constraints and investment fluctuations: an empirical investigation", in R.G. Hubbard (ed.) *Financial Markets and Financial Crises*, University of Chicago Press.

Gilchrist, S. and Himmelberg, C.P. (1995) "Evidence on the role of cash-flow for investment", *Journal of Monetary Economics*, 36, 541–572.

Goffee, R. and Scase R. (1983) "Business ownership and women's subordination", *Sociological Review* vol. 31, November 1983.

Goldberg, L.G. and White, L.J. (1998) "De novo banks and lending to small businesses: an empirical analysis", *Journal of Banking and Finance* 22, 851–867.

Golinelli, R. and Monterastelli, M. (1990) Un metodo per la ricostruzione di serie storiche compatibili con la nuova Contabilita' Nazionale, Nota di lavoro, n. 9001, Prometeia, Bologna.

Graziani, A. (1992) L'economia Italiana dal Dopoguerra ad Oggi, ESI, Naples, Italy.

Greene, P.G., Brush, C.G., Hart, M.M. and Saparito, P. (2001) "Patterns of venture capital funding: is gender a factor?" *Venture Capital* 3(1), 63–83.

Greene, W.H. (1993) *Econometric Analysis*, Macmillan.

Greenwald, B. and Stiglitz, J. (1988) "Financial market imperfections and business fluctuations", *Quarterly Journal of Economics* 108, 77–114.

Greenwald, B., Stiglitz, J.E. and Weiss, A. (1984) "Informational imperfections in the capital markets and macroeconomic fluctuation", *American Economic Review* 74, 194–200.

Greenwood, J. and Williamson, S.D. (1989) "International financial intermediation and aggregate fluctuations under alternative exchange rate regimes", *Journal of Monetary Economics* 23, 401–431.

Grosskopf, S. (1986) "The role of the reference technology in measuring technical efficiency", *Economic Journal* 96, 499–513.

Grosskopf, S. (1993) "Efficiency and productivity", in H. Fried, C.A.K. Lovell and P. Schmidt(eds) *The Measurement of Productive Efficiency*, OUP.

Grosskopf, S., Hayes, K., Taylor, L. and Weber, W. (1996) "Budget constrained frontier measures of fiscal equality and efficiency in schooling", *Review of Economics and Statistics* 79, 116–124.

Hailu, G., Jeffery, S.R. and Goddard, E.W. (2007) "Efficiency, economic performance and financial leverage of agribusiness marketing co-operatives in Canada", in *Global Market: Incidence, Viability and Economic Performance, Advances in the Economic Analysis of Participatory and Labour-Managed Firms*, vol. 10, 47–80.

Haines, G.H., Orser, B.J. and Riding, A.L. (1999) "Myths and realities: an empirical study of banks and the gender of small business clients", *Canadian Journal of Administrative Sciences* 16(4), 291–307.

Hamilton, B.H. (2000) "Does entrepreneurship pay? An empirical analysis of the returns to self employment", *Journal of Political Economy* 108, 604–631.

Hamilton, R.T. and Fox, M.A. (1998) "The financing preferences of small firm owners", *International Journal of Entrepreneurial Behaviour and Research* 4(3), 239–248.

Harding, R. (2004) Global Entrepreneurship Monitor, London Business School, United Kingdom.

Hart, Oliver (1995) *Firms, Contracts and Financial Structure*, Oxford: Clarendon Press.

Haskel, J. and Sanchis, A. (2000) "A barganing model of Farrell inefficiency", *International Journal of Industrial Organisation* vol. 18, no. 4, March, 539–556.

Hausman, J.A. (1978) "Specification tests in econometrics", *Econometrica* 46, 1215–1271.

Hay, Donald A. and Liu, G.S. (1997) "The efficiency of firms: what difference does competition make?" *Economic Journal* 107, (May), 597–617.

Hayashi, F. and Inoue, T. (1991) "The relation between firm growth and Q with multiple capital goods: theory and evidence from panel data on Japanese firms", *Econometrica* 59, 731–53.

Haynes, G.W. and Haynes, D.C. (1999) "The debt structure of small businesses owned by women in 1987 and 1993", *Journal of Small Business Management* 37(2), 1–19.

Hellwig, M. (1986) "Comments on 'The pure theory of country risk' by J. Eaton, M. Gersovitz and J. Stiglitz", *European Economic Review* 30: 3, 521–527.

Hermalin, B.E. (1992) "The effects of competition on executive behavior", *Rand Journal of Economics*, The RAND Corporation, vol. 23(3), 350–365.

Hisrich, R.D. and Brush, C.G. (1984) "The woman entrepreneur: management skills and business problems", *Journal of Small Business Management* 22(1), 30–37.

Hisrich, R.D. and Brush, C.G. (1986) *"The Woman Entrepreneur: Starting, Financing, and Managing a Successful New Business"*, Lexington, MA: Lexington Books, Inc.

Hisrich, R.D. and O'Brien, M. (1982) "The woman entrepreneur from a business and sociological perspective", in K.H. Vesper (ed.) *Frontiers of Entrepreneurship Research*, pp. 54–77, Wellesley, MA: Babson College.

Holtz-Eakin, D., Joulfaian, D. and Rosen, H.S. (1994) "Entrepreneurial decisions and liquidity constraints", *Rand Journal of Economics* 25, 334–347.

Hoshi, T., Kashyap, A. and Scharfstein, D. (1991) "Corporate structure, liquidity and investment: evidence from Japanese industrial groups", *Quarterly Journal of Economics* 90, 33–61.

Hout, M. and Rosen, H.S. (2000) "Self-employment, family background, and race", *Journal of Human Resources* 35, 670–692.

Howorth, C.A. (2001) "Small firms' demand for finance", *International Small Business Journal* 19(4), 78–86.

Hubbard, G.R. and Kashyap, A.K. (1992) "Internal net worth and the investment process: an application to US agriculture", *Journal of Political Economy* 100, 506–534.

Hubbard, G.R., Kashyap, A.K. and Whited, T. (1995) "Internal finance and firm Invest-ment", *Journal of Money, Credit and Banking* 27, 683–701.

Huffman, W.E. (2001) "Human capital: education and agriculture", in Gardner, B.L. and Rausser, G.C. (eds) *Handbook of Agricultural Economics*, Amsterdam: Elsevier Science.

Hughes, M.D. (1988) "A stochastic frontier cost function for residential child care provi-sion", *Journal of Applied Econometrics*, vol. 3, 203–214.

INEA (2001) *Annuario dell'agricoltura italiana*, Napoli: Edizioni Scientifiche Italiane.

Irwin, D. and Scott, J.M. (2006) The Barriers Faced by SMEs in Raising Finance from Banks, paper presented at the ISBE conference, November, Cardiff.

ISMEA (2002) Filiera vino, Roma.

ISTAT (2002) Numeri indici dei prezzi alla produzione e al consumo, Collana Infor-mazioni, no. 54, Roma.

Johnson, S. and Storey, D. (1993) *Women Entrepreneurs*, London: Routledge.

Jondrow, J., Lovell, C.A.K., Materov, I.S. and Schmidt, P. (1982) "On the estimation of technical inefficiency in the stochastic frontier production function model", *Journal of Econometrics* 19: 2/3, 233–238.

Jones, D. and Svejnar, J. (1985) "Participation, profit sharing, worker ownership and effi-ciency in Italian producer cooperatives", *Economica* 52 (208), 449–465.

Jones, D., Klinedinst, M. and Rock, C. (1998) "Productive efficiency during transition: evidence from Bulgarian panel data", *Journal of Comparative Economics* 26, 446–464.

Jones, E. (2001) "The industrial finance department: an Australian experiment in small business finance", *Australian Economic History Review* 41(2), 176–197.

Jorgenson, D.W. (1970) "The predictive performance of econometric models of quarterly investment behavior", *Econometrica* 38, 213–224.

Kodde, D.A. and Palm, F.C. (1986) "Wald criteria for jointly testing equality and inequality restrictions", *Econometrica* 54(5), 1243–1248.

Koopmans, T.C. (1951) "An analysis of production as an efficient combination of activ-ities", in T.C. Koopmans (ed.) *Activity Analysis of Production and Allocation*, Cowles Commission for Research in Economics, Monograph 13, New York: Wiley.

Koper, G. (1993) "Women entrepreneurs and the granting of business credit", in Allen, S. and Truman, C. (eds), *Women in Business: Perspectives on Women Entrepreneurs*, London: Routledge.

Kotey, B. (1999) "Debt financing and factors internal to the business", *International Small Business Journal* 17(3), 11–29.

Kumbhakar, S.C. (1990) "Production frontiers, panel data and time-varying technical inefficiency, *Journal of Econometrics* 46(1/2), 201–211.

Kumbhakar, S.C. and Lovell, C.A.K. (2000) *Stochastic Frontier Analysis*, Cambridge and New York: Cambridge University Press.

Kwon, E. (2000) "Factor demands, effective discount rates, and liquidity constraints in the retail trade firm", *Economic Inquiry* 38(2), 304–319.

Lega delle Cooperative (2006) Internationalisation of Cooperatives: Some Experiences and Reflections by Legacoop, mimeo, Rome, Italy.

Lindh, T. and Ohlsson, H. (1996) "Self-employment and windfall gains: evidence from the Swedish lottery", *Economic Journal* 106, 1515–1526.

Lindh, T. and Ohlsson, H. (1998) "Self-employment and wealth inequality", *Review of Income and Wealth*, 44, 25–42.

Lombard, K.V. (2001) "Female self-employment and demand for flexible, non-standard work schedules", *Economic Inquiry* 39, 214–237.

Lombardi, P. and Mele, M. (1993) "Indagine sulla performance di un campione di cantine sociali che non effettua l'imbottigliamento attraverso diverse metodologie di analisi", in Pacciani, A., Petriccione, G. (eds), *La cooperazione agro-alimentare in Italia*, Bologna: Il Mulino.

Loscocco, K. and Smith-Hunter, A. (2004) "Women home-based business owners: insights from comparative analysis", *Women in Management Review* 19(3), 164–173.

Maietta, O.W. and Sena, V. (2004) "Profit-sharing, technical efficiency change and financial constraints", in *Employee Participation, Firm Performance and Survival*, v. 8, Elsevier.

Maietta, O.W. and Sena, V. (2007) "Organizational capital, product market competition and technical efficiency in Italian cooperatives", in *Cooperative Firms in Global Market: Incidence, Viability and Economic Performance, Advances in the Economic Analysis of Participatory and Labour-Managed Firms*, v. 10, 29–46.

Martin, S. (1993) "Endogenous firm efficiency in a Cournot principal-agent model", *Journal of Economic Theory* 59, 445–450.

Mediocredito Centrale (1997) Indagine sulle Imprese Manifatturiere. Sesto Rapporto sull'Industria Italiana e sulla Politica Industriale, Roma.

Meesun, W. and van den Broeck, J. (1977) "Efficiency estimation from Cobb–Douglas production functions with composed error", *International Economic Review* 18(2), 435–444.

Merrett, C.D. and Gruidl, J.J. (2000) "Small business ownership in Illinois: the effect of gender and location on entrepreneurial success", *Professional Geographer* 52, 425–436.

Meyer, L.H. (1998) "The present and future roles of banks in small business finance", *Journal of Banking and Finance* 22(7), 1109–1116.

Minniti, M., Arenius, P. and Langowitz, N. (2004) *Global Monitor Entrepreneurship – 2004 Report on Women and Entrepreneurship*, Wellesley, Mass: Babson College and London Business School (The Center for Women's Leadership).

Morrison, C. (1993) *A Microeconomic Approach to the Measurement of Economic Performance: Productivity Growth, Capacity Utilization and Related Performance Indicators*, New York: Springer Verlag.

Morrison, C. and Diewert, W.E. (1990) "New techniques in the measurement of multifactor productivity", *Journal of Productivity Analysis* 1(4), 267–286.

Mosheim, R. (2002) "Organizational type and efficiency in the Costa Rican coffee processing sector", *Journal of Comparative Economics* 30, 296–316.

Nakamura, A. and Nakamura, M. (1981) "On the relationships among several specification error tests presented by Durbin, Wu and Hausman", *Econometrica* 49(6), 1583–1588.

Ng, S. and Schaller, H. (1996) "The risky spread, investment and monetary policy transmission: evidence on the role of asymmetric information", *Review of Economics and Statistics* 375–383.

Nickell, S. and Nicolitsas, D. (1999) "How does financial pressure affect firms", *European Economic Review* 43, 1435–1456.

Nickell, S., Nicolitsas, D. and Dryden, N. (1997) "What makes firms perform well", *European Economic Review* 43, 783–796.

Nickell, S.J. (1996) "Competition and corporate performance", *Journal of Political Economy* 104: 4, 724–745.

Nilsson, P. (1997) "Business counseling directed towards female entrepreneurs some legitimacy dilemmas", *Entrepreneurship and Regional Development* 9(3), 239–257.

Nishimizu, M. and Page, J.M. (1982) "Total factor productivity growth, technological progress and technical efficiency change: dimensions of productivity change in Yugoslavia 1965–78", *Economic Journal* 92, 920–936.

OECD (1998) *Women Entrepreneurs in Small and Medium Enterprises* (Paris and Washington, DC: OECD).

Olm, K., Carsrud, A.L. and Alvey, L. (1988) "The role of networks in new venture funding of female entrepreneurs: a continuing analysis", in Kirchoff, B.A., Long, W.A., McMullan, E., Vesper, K.H. and Wetzel, W.E. (eds) *Frontiers of Entrepreneurship Research*, Wellesley, MA: Babson College.

Orser, B., Hogarth-Scott, S. and Riding, A. (2000) "Performance, firm size, and management problem solving", *Journal of Small Business Management* 38(4), 42–58.

Orser, B., Riding, A. and Swift, C. (1994) "Banking experiences of Canadian microbusiness", *Journal of Enterprising Culture* 2(1), 1–10.

Pagano, U. (1992) "Organizational equilibria and production efficiency", *Metroeconomica* 43: 1–2, 227–246.

Pellegrino, E.T. and Reese, B.L. (1982) "Perceived formative and operational problems encountered by women entrepreneurs in retail and service firms", *Journal of Small Business Management* 20(2), 15–24.

Pencavel, J., Pistaferri, L. and Schivardi, F. (2005) Wages, Employment and Capital in Capitalist and Worker-Owned Firms, mimeo, University of Stanford.

Perelman, S. and Pestieu, P. (1988) "Technical performance in public enterprise: a comparative study of railways and postal services", *European Economic Review* 32, 432–441.

Perotin, V. and Robinson, A. (1998) "Profit-sharing and productivity: evidence from Britain, France, Germany and Italy", *Advances in the Economic Analysis of Participatory and Labor-Managed Firms* 6, 135–160.

Pindyck, R.S. and Rotemberg, J. (1983) "Dynamic factor demands under rational expectations", *Scandinavian Journal of Economics* 85, 223–238.

Pitt, M.M. and Lee, L.F. (1981) Measurement and sources of technical inefficiency in the Indonesian weaving industry", *Journal of Development Economics* 9, 43–64.

Porter, P. and Scully, G.W. (1987) "Economic efficiency in cooperatives", *Journal of Law and Economics* 30 (October), 489–512.

Poterba, J. and Summers, L.H. (1983) "Dividend tax corporate investment and Q", *Journal of Public Economics* 22: 3, 135–167.

Presser, H.B. (1995) "Job, family, and gender: determinants of non-standard work schedules among employed Americans in 1991", *Demography* 32, 577–598.

Rees, H. and Shah, A. (1986) "An empirical analysis of self-employment in the UK", *Journal of Applied Econometrics* 1, 95–108.

Renzulli, L., Aldrich, H. and Moody, J. (2000) "Family matters: gender, networks and entrepreneurial outcomes", *Social Forces* 79, 523–546.

Richmond, J. (1974) "Estimating the efficiency of production, *International Economic Review* 15(2), 515–521.

Riding, A.L. and Swift, C.S. (1990) "Women business owners and the terms of credit: some empirical findings of the Canadian experience", *Journal of Business Venturing* 5(5), 327–340.

Riley, J.C. (1987) "Credit rationing: a further remark", *American Economic Review* 77, 224–227.

Robb, A. and Wolken, J. (2002) "Firm, owner and financing characteristics: Differences between female- and male-owned small businesses" Finance and Economics Discussion series, Division of Research and Statistics and Monetary Affairs, Federal Reserve Board, Washington D. C., 18.

Rosa, P., Hamilton, D., Carter, S. and Burns, H. (1994) "The impact of gender on small business management: preliminary findings of a British study", *International Small Business Journal* 12(3), 25–32.

Schaller, H. (1990) "A re-examination of the Q Theory of Investment using U.S. firm data", *Journal of Applied Econometrics* 5, 309–325.

Schaller, H. (1993) "Asymmetric information, liquidity constraints and Canadian investment", *Canadian Journal of Economics* 26, 552–574.

Schiantarelli, F. (1996) "Financial constraints and investment: methodological issues and international evidence", *Oxford Review of Economic Policy* 12, 70–89.

Schiantarelli, F. and Georgoutsos, D. (1990) "Monopolistic competition and the Q Theory of Investment", *European Economic Review* 34: 4, 1061–1078.

Schmidt-Mohr, U. (1997) "Rationing versus collateralization in competitive and monopolistic credit markets with asymmetric information", *European Economic Review* 41(7), 1321–1342.

Schmidt, P. and Lovell, C.A.K. (1979) "Estimating technical and allocative inefficiency relative to stochastic production and cost frontiers", *Journal of Econometrics* 9, 343–366.

Schmidt, P. and Sickles, R.C. (1984) "Production frontiers and panel data", *Journal of Business and Economic Statistics* 2, 367–374.

Schwartz, E.B. (1979) "Entrepreneurship: a new female frontier", *Journal of Contemporary Business* 4, 47–76.

Scott, C.E. (1986) "Why more women are becoming entrepreneurs?" *Journal of Small Business Management* 24(4), 37–44.

Scott, M.F.G. (1991) *A New Theory of Economic Growth*, Oxford: Oxford University Press.

Sessions, J. (1992) Profit-Sharing and Gift Exchange Efficiency Wage, Loughborough University Discussion Paper, 11.

Siegel, D. (1995) "Errors of measurement and the recent acceleration in manufacturing productivity growth", *Journal of Productivity Analysis* 6(4), 297–320.

Small Business Service (2004) "SBS Household Survey of Entrepreneurship 2003", April.

Stevenson, L.A. (1986) "Against all odds: the entrepreneurship of women", *Journal of Small Business Management* 24(3), 30–36.

Stevenson, R.E. (1980) "Likelihood functions for generalized stochastic frontier estimation", *Journal of Econometrics* 13(1), 58–66.

Stiglitz, J. and Weiss, A. (1981) "Credit rationing in markets with imperfect information", *American Economic Review*, 71: 3, 393–410.

Stiglitz, J.E. and Weiss, A. (1985) Credit Rationing and Collateral, Bell Communications Research Discussion Paper.

Stiglitz, J.E. and Weiss, A. (1987) "Credit rationing: reply", *American Economic Review* 77, 228–231.

Storey, D. (1994) "New firm growth and bank financing", *Small Business Economics*, 6(2), 139–150.

Storey, D.J. (2004) "Racial and gender discrimination in the micro firms credit market? Evidence from Trinidad and Tobago", *Small Business Economics* 23, 401–422.

Strahan, P.E. and Weston, J.P. (1998) "Small business lending and the changing structure of the banking industry", *Journal of Banking and Finance* 22(7), 821–845.

Taylor, M.P. (1996) "Earnings, independence, or unemployment: why become self-employed?" *Oxford Bulletin of Economics and Statistics* 58, 253–266.

Treichel, M.Z. and Scott, J.A. (2006) "Women-owned businesses and access to bank credit: evidence from three surveys since 1987", *Venture Capital* 8(1), 51–67.

Uvalic M. (1991) The Pepper Report: Promotion of Employee Participation in

Profits and Enterprise Results in Member States of the European Community, Luxembourg.

Uzzi, B. (1999) "Embeddedness in the making of financial capital: how social relations and the networks benefit firms seeking financing", *American Sociological Review* 64, 481–505.

Van Auken, H.E., Gaskill, L.R. and Kao, S. (1993) "Acquisition of capital by women entrepreneurs: patterns of initial and refinancing capitalisation", *Journal of Small Business and Entrepreneurship* 10:4, 44–55.

Van Bekkum O. and van Dijk G. (1998) *Lo sviluppo delle cooperative agricole nell'Unione Europea*, Ancona: Edizioni CLUA.

Van Dijk, G. and Mackel, C. (1991) "Dutch agriculture seeking for market leader strategies", *European Review of Agricultural Economics* 18: 3–4, 345–364.

Vercammen, J.A. (1995) "Credit bureau policy and sustainable reputation effects in credit markets", *Economica* 62(248), 461–78.

Vercammen, J. (2002) "Welfare improving adverse selection in credit markets", *International Economic Review* 43, 1017–1033.

Verheul, I. and Thurik, R.A. (2001) "Start-up capital: does gender matter?" *Small Business Economics* 16, 329–345.

Vickers, J.S. (1995) "Concepts of competition", *Oxford Economic Papers*, 47 1: 1–23.

Waldman, D. (1982) "A stationary point for the stochastic frontier likelihood", *Journal of Econometrics*, 18, 275–279.

Warren-Smith, I. and Jackson, C. (2004) "Women creating wealth through rural enterprise", *International Journal of Entrepreneurial Behaviour and Research*, 10: 10, 369–383.

Weiss, C. (1990) "The role of intermediaries in strengthening women's self-employment activities", in S.K. Gould and J. Parzen (eds) *Enterprising Women*, pp. 59–74, Paris: Organization for Economic Co-operation and Development.

Weitzman, M.L. (1995) "Incentive effects of profit-sharing and employee share ownership: theory and evidence", *Trends in Business Organisation*, Kiel.

Wellington, A. (2006) "Self-employment: the new solution for balancing family and career?" *Labor Economics* 13: 3, 357–386.

Whited, T.M. (1991) "Investment and financial asset accumulation", *Journal of Financial Intermediation* 307–334.

Whited, T.M. (1992) "Debt, liquidity constraints and corporate investment: evidence from panel data", *Journal of Finance* 47, 1425–1460.

Williamson, S.D. (1986) "Costly Monitoring, Financial Intermediation and Equilibrium Credit Rationing", *Journal of Monetary Economics* 18, 159–179.

Williamson, S.D. (1987a) "Costly monitoring, loan contracts and equilibrium credit rationing", *Quarterly Journal of Economics* 102, 135–146.

Williamson, S.D. (1987b) "Financial intermediation, business failures and real business cycles", *Journal of Political Economy* 95, 1196–1216.

Winker, P. (1999) "Causes and effects of financing constraints at the firm level", *Small Business Economics* 12(2), 169–181.

Wu, D. (1973) "Alternative tests of independence between stochastic regressors and disturbances", *Econometrica* 41, 733–750.

Wu, D. (1974) "Alternative tests of independence between stochastic regressors and disturbances: finite sample results", *Econometrica* 42, 529–546.

Index